Developing P

Developing Primary Science

Edited by John Sharp

Learning Matters

First published in 2004 by Learning Matters Ltd.

British Library Cataloguing in Publication Data
A CIP record for this book is available from the British Library

ISBN 1 844450 02 3

Cover design by Topics – The Creative Partnership
Project management by Deer Park Productions
Typeset by PDQ Typesetting, Newcastle under Lyme
Printed and bound by Bell & Bain Ltd, Glasgow

Learning Matters Ltd
33 Southernhay East
Exeter EXI INX
Tel: 01392 215560
Email: info@learningmatters.co.uk
www.learningmatters.co.uk

CONTENTS

Every effort has been made to contact copyright holders. In the unlikely event that permission has not been granted to reproduce figures and acknowledgement has not been made, the copyright holder should contact Learning Matters. We will then make sure that suitable acknowledgement is made in the next printing of this volume.

The following figures have been reproduced, with permission, from:

Figure 1.1 – Nott, M. and Wellington, J. (1993) Your nature of science profile: an activity for science teachers *School Science Review*, 75 (270), 109-112.

Table 1.1 – Osborne, J., Ratcliffe, M., Collins, S., Millar, R., Duschl, R. (2001) *What should we teach about science? A Delphi study*. London: King's College. Also Osborne, J., Ratcliffe, M., Collins, S., Millar, R., Duschl, R. (2003) What 'ideas- about-science' should be taught in school science? A Delphi study of the expert community. *Journal of Research in Science Teaching* 40 (7), 692-720.

Tables 1.2 and 1.3 – Driver, R., Leach, J., Millar, R., Scott, P. (1996) *Young People 's Images of Science*. Buckingham: Open University Press.

Figure 1.2 – Bartholomew, H., Osborne, J. and Ratcliffe, M. (2004) Teaching pupils 'ideas- about-science': five dimensions of effective practice. *Science Education* (In press).

Figure 2.3 – Russell, T. and Watt, D. (1990) *Growth*, SPACE Project Research Report. Liverpool: Liverpool University Press.

Figure 2.4 – Osborne, J., Black, P., Smith, M. and Meadows, J. (1990) *Light*, SPACE Project Research Report. Liverpool: Liverpool University Press.

Figure 2.5 – Watt, D. and Russell, T. (1990) *Sound*, SPACE Project Research Report. Liverpool: Liverpool University Press.

Figure 2.6 – research projects of Vicky Dray and Lucy Clarke (former undergraduate students at the University of Plymouth).

Figure 7.1 – Russell, T., Longden, K. and McGuigan, L. (1991) *Materials*, Primary SPACE Project Research Report. Liverpool: Liverpool University Press.

Figures 7.2 and 7.3 – Naylor, S. and Keogh, B. (2000) *Concept Cartoons in Science Education*. Cheshire: Millgate House Publishers.

Figure 7.4 – Johnson, P. (1998) Progression in children's understanding of a 'basic' particle theory: a longitudinal study. *International Journal of Science Education*, 20 (4), 393-412.

Figure 8.2 – Kibble, B. (2002) How do you picture electricity? *Primary Science Review*, 74, 28-30.

Figure 8.3 – Daehler, K. R. and Shinohara, M. (2001) A complete circuit is a complete circle: exploring the potential of case materials and methods to develop teachers' content knowledge and pedagogical content knowledge of science. *Research in Science Education*, 31:2, 267-288.

Figure 8.7 – Vaz, S. (1998) Sam feels the force. *Primary Science*. Hatfield: Association for Science Education.

Chapter 5 – The Science Curriculum is drawn from an article soon to appear in *Research Papers in Education* and reproduced, with permission, from Taylor and Francis.

About this book

Walk up to the education section in any bookstore and you'll find a bewildering array of texts addressing very many different aspects of primary science. If you had to categorise them, however, at least three different sorts would probably emerge. There are those that deal almost exclusively with subject knowledge, those that deal almost exclusively with pedagogy and the practicalities of teaching science, and those that deal almost exclusively with science in more philosophical or theoretical terms. Here, we have attempted the impossible and tried to bring something from all three sorts together. We have done this in order to provide an informative and up-to-date account of what we believe teachers of primary science should know about, particularly in today's climate of persistent educational challenge and change.

Features of this book include:

- **relevance to both pre-service and in-service education and training needs;**
- **strategies for self-analysis and the promotion of critical reflection as a means of improving professional practice in context;**
- **the integration of subject, pedagogical and curricular knowledge for effective teaching and learning;**
- **the application and use of both experience and evidence-based research;**
- **clear links building on Science in the National Curriculum at Key Stages I and 2.**

Intended audience

When we set out to write this book we had very different audiences in mind. In the first instance, it will be of direct interest to primary trainees on all courses of initial teacher training and education in England and other parts of the UK where a secure knowledge of science in its many forms is required for the award of Qualified Teacher Status (QTS). For trainees, however, this book is not a first reader. Instead, we see it being used most by more experienced individuals in the final years of undergraduate programmes as well as generalists and specialists following postgraduate routes. This book will also be of direct interest to those pursuing educational studies as a major or minor pathway and all teachers, mentors and curriculum leaders looking to develop their science teaching either by themselves or on courses of continuing professional development offered by local education authorities and Science Learning Centres.

Chapter details

This book falls almost naturally into two distinct parts. The first part, which includes Chapters I to 5, deals with aspects of primary science which are either almost 'taken for granted' these days or rarely receive the attention they deserve. In the latter case, the nature of science, the issue of teachers' curricular expertise and the history and evolution of the science curriculum make for essential reading. Knowledge and understanding and acquiring scientific skills in particular set the scene for the second part and Chapters 6, 7 and 8, the science most familiar as life processes and living things, materials and physical processes. Of course, each chapter is not a discrete entity in its own right and some examples, particularly from the conceptually difficult areas of physical processes, are encountered on more than one occasion. The chapters themselves have been written by a number of experienced science educators, each with a strong primary background, and each committed to improving the quality of science education provision nationwide.

Contributors

Mary Ratcliffe is a professor in education at the University of Southampton. Before this she taught chemistry and general science in schools in East Anglia. Mary's current interests are in reactions to socio-scientific issues, the understanding of the nature of science and the development of effective learning and assessment practice.

Joan Parker is a professor in education at Manchester Metropolitan University. She has worked as both a research scientist in the field of ecology as well as being a primary school teacher in Trafford. Joan's current interest is concerned with the development of subject and pedagogical content knowledge in the training and continuing professional development of teachers.

Anne Goldsworthy taught for many years in a variety of primary schools. She is now an independent consultant for science providing INSET throughout the UK and overseas. She has written numerous articles and books and was a member of the AKSIS (Association for Science Education – King's College Science Investigation) project. Anne has a particular interest in scientific enquiry.

Dave Heywood is a lecturer in science education at Manchester Metropolitan University. A former deputy head teacher, he has worked in both primary and secondary schools in the north of England. Dave's current interest is focused on how best to support teachers in developing their subject and pedagogical content knowledge in the training and continuing professional development of teachers.

John Sharp is a principal lecturer in education studies at Bishop Grosseteste College in Lincoln. He previously taught science at the University of Southampton and science and geography at the University of Plymouth. John's current interests are concerned with children's cognitive development in science, particularly in the areas of Earth and space, and the curriculum.

Rob Bowker is a lecturer in primary science at the University of Exeter. Before this he worked in primary and middle schools in the south-west of England as a teacher and later as a deputy head. Rob's current interests focus on the teaching and learning of science within non-school contexts such as the Eden Project in Cornwall.

Jenny Byrne is a lecturer in science education at the University of Southampton. Before this she taught in primary and secondary schools and worked as a local education authority advisor. Jenny's current interests include children's ideas about micro-organisms, health education and the sustained recruitment of students to initial teacher training.

Marcus Grace is a lecturer in science education and environmental education at the University of Southampton. Before this he taught biology and general science at schools in London. Marcus's current interests are in young people's views of biological conservation issues and the science underpinning education for citizenship.

Frankie McKeon is a lecturer in science education at the University of Leicester. Before this she taught in a variety of Leicestershire schools. Frankie's current interests include children's and adults' conceptual development in science and the development of appropriate teaching and learning strategies.

Graham Peacock is a lecturer in primary science at Sheffield Hallam University. Before this he taught across the entire primary and secondary age range. He has written a number of books and articles for teachers and children and provides INSET throughout the UK. Graham's current interests lie in helping trainees develop their subject and pedagogical content knowledge in physical processes.

Robin Smith is a lecturer in science education at Sheffield Hallam University. For many years he has taught children, students and teachers and he has published widely to support the development of primary science. Robin's current interests include helping teachers and trainees develop their subject and pedagogical content knowledge .

1 NATURE OF SCIENCE
MARY RATCLIFFE

Introduction

Few primary teachers ever receive a formal education in the nature of science, that is an in-depth study of its history and philosophy and a chance to examine the many different views on its purpose and practice. Indeed, most tend to gain an understanding of the nature of science implicitly through their own professional experiences or science as practised in higher education or industry. Seldom is that understanding made explicit either by reflection or formal evaluation. Of course, controversy surrounds the nature of science and some philosophers spend their entire working lives examining just exactly what it is. It is perhaps not surprising, therefore, that many teachers are considered to hold views about the nature of science that at best are naive (Abd-El-Khalick and Lederman, 2000). Thinking about the nature of science, however, promotes debate about what is important in children's science education. This chapter explores views on teaching and learning about the nature of science and its relevance to primary education.

What is science?

The word science comes from the Latin *scientia* meaning 'knowledge'. So literally, science is about knowing about the world. Over the centuries, different views on how we best come to know about the natural and physical world and the status of that knowledge have emerged. Primary science, for example, is often regarded as an intellectual, practical, creative and social endeavour which seeks to help children better understand and make sense of the world in which they live by involving them in thinking and working in particular ways in the pursuit of reliable knowledge (Sharp et al., 2002). However, science and primary science mean different things to different people.

There are some aspects of terminology related to the nature of science that are worth exploring here to put the subsequent discussion into context. Nott and Wellington (1993) developed a useful exercise for teachers to allow them to reflect on their view of the nature of science. In this exercise, agreeing or disagreeing with such statements as 'There is such a thing as a true scientific theory' and 'Human emotion plays no part in the creation of scientific knowledge' allows a nature of science profile to be drawn which can be compared against others. Underpinning this exercise are a number of dimensions along which teachers position themselves. These reflect some of the terminologies and concepts relevant to the nature of science and its teaching (see also Chalmers, 1978 and Dunbar, 1995). A summary relating to the nature of science and the extremes of Nott and Wellington's dimensions is provided (Figure 1.1).

Other researchers have developed different instruments for collecting and evaluating teachers' views on the nature of science (e.g. Cotham and Smith, 1981, with a questionnaire and subscales relating to different aspects of the nature of science, and

Positivist
Science is the primary source of truth. The laws and theories generated by experiments are descriptions of patterns in a real, external objective world.

Relativist
Judgements as to the truth of scientific theories vary from individual to individual and from one culture to another, i.e. truth is relative not absolute.

Inductivist
According to inductivism, scientists generalise from a set of observations to a universal law 'inductively', inferring from the particular to the general. Scientific knowledge is built by induction from a secure set of observations.

Deductivist
According to deductivism, scientists form hypotheses which are not established by the empirical data but may be suggested by them. Science then proceeds by testing the observable consequences of these hypotheses, i.e. observations are theory laden.

Decontextualist
Holds the view that scientific knowledge is *independent* of its cultural location and sociological structure.

Contextualist
Holds the view that the truth of scientific knowledge and processes is *interdependent* with the culture in which the scientists live and in which it takes place.

Realist
Believes that scientific theories are statements about a world that exists in space and time independent of the scientists' perceptions. Correct theories describe things which are really there, independent of the scientists (e.g. atoms).

Instrumentalist
Believes that scientific theories and ideas are fine if they work, that is they allow correct predictions to be made. They are instruments which we can use but they say nothing about an independent reality or their own truth.

Content is important
You think that science is characterised by the facts and ideas it has and that the essential part of science education is the acquisition and mastery of this 'body of knowledge'.

Process is important
You see science as a characteristic set of identifiable methods/processes. The learning of these is the essential part of science education.

Figure 1.1. Some dimensions and terminology relating to the nature of science (from Nott and Wellington, 1993)

Lederman and O'Malley, 1990, with a survey using open responses to some key questions). Research into teachers' understanding of the nature of science has shown that most are rather inconsistent in their beliefs (Abd-El-Khalick and Lederman, 2000). Although there is no one correct view of the nature of science, some are regarded as more refined than others. A mature understanding of the nature of science, for example, recognises the tentative nature of some scientific knowledge and considers positivism as inadequate.

From a review of the different positions on the nature of science, Driver *et al.* (1996) suggest that the following ideas command broad consensus:

- **Scientific enquiry involves the collection of data (evidence). This may be used to provide the 'raw material' which an explanation has to account for or to test proposed explanations.**
- **Scientific explanations are based upon generalisations (laws) and theoretical models (theories).**
- **Laws and theories are always underdetermined by data. That is, proposing a law or a theory always involves an element of uncertainty. They are inevitably conjectural.**
- **Choices between competing theories are based on criteria such as accuracy of prediction, consistency and coherence, breadth of scope, simplicity and fruitfulness in suggesting lines of enquiry. Judgement is, however, involved in deciding how these apply to any given case.**

These ideas might also be considered a concise summary of a level of understanding of the nature of science that could be possible to achieve during formal science education throughout the primary years and beyond.

Pause for thought

What are your views on the nature of science?

McComas (1998) explodes several myths about the nature of science. Here is an example. A common misconception is that theories, developed from hypotheses, can become laws with more empirical evidence – i.e. a theory is more tentative than a law. In fact, laws and theories are different kinds of knowledge. Laws are generalisations or patterns in nature (e.g. Newton's laws of force and motion). Theories are explanations of such generalisations (e.g. Darwin's theory of evolution). Do you have a refined or a naive view of the nature of science?

To give an idea of recent disputes concerning the nature of science and the relevance for teaching, it is worth considering the articles and discussions in a leading science education journal. Alters (1997a), himself a philosopher of science, undertook a survey of 187 fellow philosophers to examine their views on the nature of science. He found that there was considerable disagreement among these individuals on specific details and a general disagreement with the tenets of the nature of science as expressed in science education documents in particular. He argued that teachers should adopt a philosophically pluralistic approach in teaching, acknowledging the diversity of opinion currently available. Science educators reacted to Alters' article by arguing that his research was flawed, that there was in fact refined understanding and consensus among science educators, and that teachers would have difficulty in adopting a pluralistic approach as their understanding of the nature of science was insufficiently developed (Smith *et al.*, 1997). Alters (1997b) counter-attacked by defending the quality of his research and reiterating the need for a pluralistic approach. While this debate may seem esoteric, it illustrates the contention surrounding the nature of science and its teaching. Is there anything that can help guide a realistic approach to what should be taught?

What should be taught about the nature of science?

Aspects of the nature of science are embedded in the National Curriculum in England (DfEE/QCA, 1999) and in other curricula around the world with themes and wording apparently being established through consensus and compromise. The means by which the National Curriculum was developed are not transparent but involved consultation with teachers, learned associations and researchers. There are pragmatic elements in revising national curricula, building on what has gone before. But if we were to start with a blank sheet, what should be taught about the nature of science, its processes and practices?

This question was explored as part of a major research project by seeking the views of a range of experts through a Delphi study (Osborne *et al.* 2001, 2003). A Delphi study is the name given to a particular methodology for determining or establishing consensus among experts in a field. The technique is named after the oracle at Delphi in Ancient Greece where people would present sacrifices to hear expert advice! Here, the aim of the study was to examine the extent of consensus about what should be taught about the nature of science rather than consensus about the nature of science itself.

A Delphi study proceeds in stages. The first stage involves an open-ended questionnaire. The subsequent stages seek to establish points of commonality and difference among participants by researchers collating the individual views initially and returning these to all participants for further comment. Each participant is not aware of who the other participants are until the end of the research to allow equal weighting to be given to all views. The participants in this study were 25 people with acknowledged expertise in communicating and using or researching the processes and practices of science. These included leading scientists, historians, philosophers and sociologists of science, primary and secondary teachers of science and science educators.

In the first stage, each participant was asked to complete an open-ended questionnaire which asked what, if anything, should be taught about the methods of science, the nature of scientific knowledge and the institutions and social practices of science? Individual responses were collated, categorised into 30 themes and returned to all participants for the second stage. Participants then rated the importance of each theme for inclusion in the science curriculum and were asked to justify their rating. The 18 most highly rated themes from the second stage formed the basis for the final stage in which participants rated each theme again, based on what they thought should be taught *explicitly*.

Nine themes emerged with strong consensus (Table 1.1). This work showed that people with differing views on the nature of science could agree on an account of the nature

---

Nature of scientific knowledge
Science and certainty
Students should appreciate why much scientific knowledge, particularly that taught in school science, is well-established and beyond reasonable doubt, and why other scientific knowledge is more open to legitimate doubt. It should be explained that current scientific knowledge is the best we have but may be subject to change in the future, given new evidence or new interpretations of old evidence.

Historical development of scientific knowledge
Students should be taught some of the historical background to the development of scientific knowledge.

Methods of science
Scientific methods and critical testing
Students should be taught that science uses the experimental method to test ideas and, in particular, should be about certain basic techniques such as the use of controls. It should be made clear that the outcome of a single experiment is rarely sufficient to establish a knowledge claim.

Analysis and interpretation of data
Students should be taught that the practice of science involves skilful analysis and interpretation of data. Scientific knowledge claims do not emerge simply from the data but through a process of interpretation and theory building that can require sophisticated skills. It is possible for scientists legitimately to come to different interpretations of the same data, and therefore to disagree.

Hypothesis and prediction
Students should be taught that scientists develop hypotheses and predictions about natural phenomena. This process is essential to the development of new knowledge claims.

Diversity of scientific thinking
Students should be taught that science uses a range of methods and approaches and that there is no one scientific method or approach.

Science and questioning
Students should be taught that an important aspect of the work of a scientist is the continual and cyclical process of asking questions and seeking answers which then lead to new questions. This process leads to the emergence of new scientific theories and techniques which are then tested empirically.

Creativity
Students should appreciate that science is an activity that involves creativity and imagination as much as many other human activities, and that some scientific ideas are enormous intellectual achievements. Scientists, as much as any other profession, are passionate and involved humans whose work relies on inspiration and imagination.

Institutions and social practices in science
Cooperation and collaboration in the development of scientific knowledge
Students should be taught that scientific work is a communal and competitive activity. While individuals may make significant contributions, scientific work is often carried out in groups, frequently of a multidisciplinary and international nature. New knowledge claims are generally shared and, to be accepted by the community, must survive a process of critical peer review.

Table 1.1 Themes forming a consensus of what should be taught *about* science
(from Osborne *et al.*, 2001, 2003)

of science that should be taught. The researchers termed this a 'vulgarised' account. Just as, for example, the model of particles as presented in the science curriculum is a simplified account of current scientific theory, so we might expect that ideas about the nature of science in the science curriculum are simplified.

Reading through these themes may show some of the similarity with the requirements of scientific enquiry in the National Curriculum in England. They also have overlap with themes in many curriculum documents around the world from McComas and Olson's (1998) analysis of curricular expectations in English-speaking countries. However, these themes go beyond current expectations of national curricula and spell out more fully what a simplified account of the nature and practices of science might contain. To adopt these themes fully requires adaptation of the science curriculum and consideration of methods of teaching – the latter issue being dealt with later in this chapter. In recent years, the nature and practices of science have become an increasing part of the National Curriculum and associated assessment yet are still probably low in teachers' thinking and priorities. Does the limited emphasis on the nature of science in current curricula matter? To address this question it is necessary to consider the purpose of learning science.

Pause for thought

Purpose of science education

If you were asked 'What do you consider the purpose of teaching science to primary school children to be?', some possible answers might include:

- *primary science provides children with a basic understanding of scientific concepts that will be built on later (a cognitive emphasis on key concepts);*
- *primary science is rooted in exploring everyday phenomena giving children practically useful knowledge (an emphasis on practical applications of science);*
- *primary science emphasises the ways in which we find out about the world, giving children an initial understanding of the nature, power and limitations of science (an emphasis on how science 'works');*
- *primary science shows the wonders of the natural and physical world (an emphasis on the affective domain).*

Depending on your answer you might emphasise or ignore the importance of the nature of science. However, ignoring it would be to deprive children of the understanding and skills required as citizens to respond critically to advances in science and social applications.

Why is the nature of science important in the science curriculum?

Scientific advancements and their applications are in the news everyday. As this chapter is being written, for example, there is considerable media debate on the safety of genetically modified (GM) crops, whether 'global warming' is happening or not and the long-term effects of mobile phone use. It is difficult to make sense of such issues and develop views on them without having some understanding of the methods of developing scientific knowledge claims and the nature of science.

Participants in the Delphi study (Osborne *et al.*, 2001, 2003) presented their arguments for the inclusion of particular themes. Some of the justifications relate to moving the emphasis from content to process, e.g. formulation of hypotheses and testing predictions are 'the spark that ignites any scientific activity' (communicator of science in Delphi study). One of the themes achieving greatest support and consensus was that of 'Science and certainty' – the recognition that scientific knowledge is open to revision. This theme was argued as important because, among other things, it highlights 'the contemporary nature of science', suggesting that there was more to be discovered. This aspect was considered important in encouraging children to think about a career in science and important for teachers to explain 'that there are certain areas where we remain largely ignorant, e.g. how the brain works'.

In *Beyond 2000*, the report drawn from a seminar series which sought to review current science education practice and to develop a framework for the future, Millar and Osborne (1998) stress the importance of education in the nature, processes and practices of science, using the term 'ideas-about-science'. This report received widespread support among the science education community and scientists, justifying considerable emphasis on 'ideas-about-science' - 'ideas about the ways in which reliable knowledge of the natural world has been, and is being, obtained'. Besides discussing the place of 'ideas-about-science', Millar and Osborne (1998) provide an interpretation of how children might gain understanding. This could come from:

- **evaluating, interpreting and analysing both evidence which has been collected first-hand and evidence which has been obtained from secondary sources;**
- **hearing and reading stories about how important ideas were first developed and became established and accepted;**
- **learning how to construct sound and persuasive arguments based upon evidence;**
- **considering a range of current issues involving the application of science and scientific ideas.**

They go on to illustrate what this might involve at different Key Stages, showing that, at Key Stages 1 and 2, children should:

- **begin to appreciate the value of measurement of quantities as a means of making a more precise record of events and processes;**
- **learn how to make simple comparisons between objects, materials and events, recognising the need to keep factors other than the one under investigation constant (making a 'fair test');**
- **become familiar with examples of scientific work which involve careful measurement and recording over a period of time (e.g. weather monitoring, testing water quality);**
- **read some non-fiction accounts of how new ideas were 'discovered', which illustrate the importance of evidence in convincing others (e.g. the circulation of the blood, microbes as the carriers of infectious diseases).**

These approaches perhaps start to show how the ideas about the nature, processes and practices of science discussed above can be made accessible to children.

Yet 'ideas-about-science' are not necessarily straightforward to teach. One particular problem arises from considering the theme of 'Science and certainty'. The body of scientific knowledge embedded in the science curriculum has been developed over centuries and is accepted as consensual knowledge or 'fact'. However, contemporary scientific endeavour results in uncertain knowledge, which is open to different inter-pretations depending on the theoretical models used and the data collection methods. Teachers are thus in a dilemma. On the one hand they have to respond to chil-dren's expectations that within the science they are studying there is a 'right' answer, particularly to assessment questions seeking understanding of fundamental concepts. Indeed, the emphasis tends to be on 'what we know' rather than 'how we know'. On the other hand, they are trying to enable children to understand the 'tentative' nature of scientific knowledge, that it is open to revision through increased and better evidence and the creativity involved in generating theoretical models. As one of the participants in the Delphi study commented: 'At one level it requires the child *not* to question school science; at another to view "frontier" science as *not* beyond question. Where does the boundary lie between those two types of science?' (Osborne *et al*., 2001, 2003). This dilemma is addressed in the sections below. It also raises questions about current knowledge of children's views about the nature of science.

What do children understand about the nature of science?

Although there are many studies which explore children's conceptions of key scientific concepts, there is far less research into children's ideas about the nature of science. One means of exploring children's ideas to good effect is via the 'draw-a-scientist' test (Chambers, 1983). Newton and Newton (1998) used this in two studies in primary schools, one in 1990 and one in 1996. In each study, the drawings of over 1,000 children were analysed to see what features were represented and whether there were changes as a result of the introduction of science into the National Curriculum. They found that children in both studies tended to draw a stereotype: a middle-aged male, bearded and in a lab coat. The scientist in most cases was indoors doing chemistry. Newton and Newton speculated as to why there was no major difference following children's more systematic exposure to science. They suggest that one reason is the lack of teaching that reflects on the nature and diverse processes of science itself.

Pause for thought

What is a scientist like?

How would you respond to the request to draw a scientist? More importantly, how do you think primary school children would respond? You could try the task out for yourself on a class and compare the results with the stereotype presented (consider perception of task as a possible bias in the work). Do your findings match those of Newton and Newton (1998)?

In more detail, Driver *et al*. (1996) used interview probes to explore the views of young people aged 9, 12 and 16 on the purposes of scientific work, the nature and status of scientific knowledge and science as a social enterprise (Table 1.2). Their probes took a variety of forms and included stories about young people discussing a 'theory' (with questions seeking views of what interviewees understood by a 'theory' and how it might be explored) and cards with different activities (with interviewees being asked to indicate whether the activity was an experiment or not and why they thought this). Driver *et al*. proposed a framework of reasoning which takes account of the responses they received to the wide variety of probes across the three ages. They identified three types of reasoning, phenomenon-based, relation-based and model-based, with phenomenon-based reasoning the most widely used form of reasoning by 9-year-olds (Table 1.3). For example, it was noted that a child who commented that scientists can find answers to the question 'Is the Earth's atmosphere heating up?' by

Activity	Comment on type of activity
This person is finding out which of the three paper towels is best at mopping up water.	Practical activity, outcome unknown, suggestion of science in context.
This person works at the post office. He is weighing parcels to decide which stamps the customer needs to buy.	Measurement, no suggestion of underpinning theory.
This person has an idea that the smaller the grains in sugar, the quicker it will dissolve in water and is testing the idea.	Empirical evaluation of formally stated hypothesis

Table 1.2. Examples of interview probes to explore the nature of an experiment (from Driver *et al*., 1996)

Form of reasoning	Form of scientific enquiry	Nature of explanation	Relationship between explanation and description
Phenomenon-based reasoning	*Focus on phenomenon* Enquiry as observation of the behaviour of the phenomenon, i.e. 'Look and see' Making phenomena happen so behaviour can be observed	*Explanation as description* Description of phenomenon; no distinction between description and explanation	*No distinction* No clear separation between description of phenomenon and explanation
Relation-based reasoning	*Correlating variables* Controlled intervention; planned observations	*Empirical generalisation* Explanation as correlational or causal	*Inductive relationship* Description and explanation distinct; explanation emerges from data; theories can be 'proved'
Model-based reasoning	*Evaluate theory* Evaluation of theory/ model in light of evidence; relationship between theory and phenomenon not straightforward	*Modelling* Theories conjectural; attempting coherence; may be multiple models/theories	*Hypothetico-deductive* Description and explanation distinct; explanations cannot be deduced from data; theories are provisional

Table 1.3. Summary of three types of young people's epistemological reasoning (from Driver *et al*., 1996)

sending people outside the Earth to see seems unable to distinguish between a description of a phenomenon and its explanation (the explanation tends to be a redescription of the phenomenon). Relation-based reasoning was the most common form of reasoning among 12- and 16-year-olds, with a few 16-year-olds demonstrating model-based reasoning. A challenge in teaching primary school children, then, may be to assist their reasoning so that they start to understand relationships between evidence and theory.

Teaching the nature of science

Most of the research exploring children's ideas about the nature of science was done before 'ideas-about-science' started to become an increasingly prominent feature of the science curriculum. Such research has shown what we might expect children to understand without explicit teaching. This final section of the chapter deals with the important issue of how explicit teaching of nature of science can be undertaken.

What most of the research instruments used for exploring teachers' understanding of the nature of science have shown is that teachers have relatively naive views of the nature of science. Does this matter? We might expect that teachers' views of the nature of science will be reflected in their general approach to teaching science and their classroom practice. For example, if your views are predominantly to the left in the dimensions shown in Figure 1.1, we might expect this to affect the way in which you teach. However, research evidence suggests that the relationship between such beliefs and action is not straightforward and that other factors dominate teaching approaches – specific curriculum imperatives, classroom management and organisation (Lantz and Kass, 1987) and pressure to cover content (Duschl and Wright, 1989), to name only a few. Certainly, we might expect that to teach the nature of science effectively a teacher needs to have a mature understanding of the nature of science.

As an extension to the Delphi study, Bartholomew et al. (2004) worked with eleven primary and secondary teachers to explore the opportunities and barriers in teaching the nature, processes and practices of science. These teachers worked with researchers in a collaborative venture to explore the issues in explicitly teaching the themes from the Delphi study (Table 1.1). Researchers presented lesson outlines in which intended learning outcomes to match particular themes were embedded in activities drawn from a number of existing sources (e.g. Lederman and Abd-El-Khalick, 1998; Ratcliffe, 1999; Goldsworthy et al., 2000; Naylor and Keogh, 2000; Feasey, 2001). Four one-day meetings helped plan and develop specific lessons related to topics that teachers knew they would be teaching. Each teacher undertook to teach at least eight lessons over a period of two terms to a target class, addressing as many of the nine themes as they felt able (Table 1.1). For the primary teachers the target class was either Year 5 or Year 6. Each teacher was visited at least three times with field notes taken of the lesson. Two of these lessons were video-taped. Teachers kept reflective diaries of their planning and teaching, and engaged in focus group discussion and individual interview at the end of the project to examine their views and actions in teaching the nature of science. In addition, children were given evaluation questionnaires after most of the lessons in order to explore what they had learnt and enjoyed.

Data analysis focused on the characteristics that distinguished effective from less effective lessons and a search for patterns.

Judgements of what constituted an effective approach were rooted in three overarching criteria: lessons should provide an opportunity for children's explicit consideration of elements of a theme, children's active engagement with the topic at hand, and the opportunity for children's dialogue which involved the construction and evaluation of reasoned arguments which related ideas to their supporting evidence. Although understanding the nature of science was one dimension of teachers' practice that proved important, it was by no means the only one – and not necessarily the most important one in enabling children to engage with 'ideas-about-science'. The analysis led to identification of a series of 'dimensions' along which the performance of the teaching of the nature of science can be distinguished (Figure 1.2). These dimensions are not mutually independent nor are they used to locate a teacher on each dimension. Rather they are an analytical tool which helps describe interrelated aspects of teaching practice in relation to the nature of science. Teachers showed a tendency to move towards the right-hand side of the dimensions as they became more confident in teaching 'ideas-about-science'.

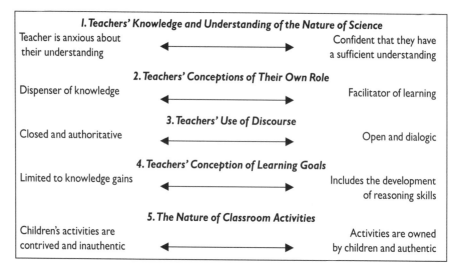

Figure 1.2. Dimensions of practice in teaching 'ideas-about-science'
(from Bartholomew *et al.*, 2004)

Within the small sample selected, the primary teachers demonstrated some key aspects of pedagogic skill in teaching the nature of science. Although they tended to lack confidence in their understanding, they were able to open up ideas to children's questioning and provide opportunity for children to explore different methods and explanations. Two examples illustrate aspects of the five dimensions and the types of activities in which they engaged. Emma and Becky (not their real names) were both able to allow Year 5 and Year 6 children to discuss 'ideas-about-science'. Emma had a degree in science and showed confidence in her understanding of the nature of science. Becky, with an arts degree, in contrast made it clear that she felt very insecure about the fact that she didn't have a scientific background and that she found her involvement in the project intimidating at times:

I didn't even do GCSE science. All these 'ideas-about-science' were very new and at first really daunting. I still don't have all the intellectual stuff behind me – and couldn't begin to teach at KS3 or 4 as I don't have the knowledge. The last lesson that was observed was on forces – the statements challenged children's ideas, but more than that, challenged my ideas because I wasn't able to explain properly why things were correct.

Nevertheless, Becky was able to use activities to allow children to exchange their own ideas and develop a questioning stance. Extracts from lessons show the opportunities for children to develop and share their ideas without being forced to the 'right answer'. The extract below is from near the beginning of Becky's lesson on insulation. Michael Rosen's poem 'Tank Jacket' has been read to the group and they are discussing the poem:

After reading, Becky asks the question 'What is the tank?'
Child 1: It's a boiler. To make the water hot.
Becky: Why does it need a jacket?
Child 1: So cold air can't get to it.
Child 2: It would hide some of the heat if you touched it by mistake.
Child 3: So it doesn't get cold.
Becky: What kind of jacket is it – what kind of material is it made of?
Someone says fabric and someone says fireproof material. Becky tells children to hold these ideas in their head and introduces a concept cartoon.

In another lesson children discussed the ways in which scientific ideas change over time:

Becky points to the board where she has written 'Do scientific ideas change?' and 'Will our scientific ideas that we have at the moment change?' Sue gives an emphatic yes straight away to the first question, but when asked to explain further is silent.
Becky: What do the rest of you think?
Tom says they do sometimes and is asked to give an example.
Tom: If you're doing an experiment on friction you might think that one thing would have more friction then you'd test it and find out that it didn't.
Becky: Very good. Jane, what do you think?
Jane: A long time ago they had different modes of transport, then the scientists thought of another way of transport, by cars.
Becky: So what's changed?
Jane: They find out new things, they find lots of things out and then they make up an idea of what they could do with it.
Becky: So, do you think that our scientific ideas – what we know now scientifically – do you think our scientific ideas will change?
She reminds them of the project they did when they learnt that people used to think the world was not a sphere. Scientists used to believe that the world was flat. Do you think that in the future scientists might change their current ideas? Jane says definitely. Becky asks why she says that and Jane says they are finding new things now. Then Michael talks about solar power and electric cars and this is picked up by Becky – the discussion gets very lively, with lots of children chipping in (e.g. 'they won't be able to drive solar power cars at

night'; 'I read something about that in a book I read for guided reading'). Becky sums up by saying that it is funny to think that maybe in 20 years' time lots of people will be driving around in solar-powered cars.

Discussions in Becky's lessons were often characterised, as in these extracts, by seeking views from a wide range of children and, while they remained rather directed by her (in that she was the one asking the questions), she tended not to evaluate responses, instead asking children to think about them. Thus, Becky opened up discussion rather than giving the 'right answer'.

Emma, with her background in science, was able at the end of the project to articulate clearly what she felt had been the main purposes and outcomes of teaching 'ideas-about-science':

> To be more explicit with the children about the process skills used in science. To give them the bigger picture as to how they all fit. To share with them that what we do is similar to what 'real' scientists do. To talk more about science and moral issues; basically taking them beyond what is perceived to be classroom science.

Emma's lessons were similar to Becky's in opening up the dialogue and giving children ownership of authentic activities. Emma had a good sense of the purpose of lessons and the difficulties she might encounter. In her diary she writes a long passage about planning for a lesson using concept cartoons and refers directly to the role she sees for herself in the lesson:

> In this lesson, after discussing hypotheses, I want them to go and make a hypothesis about the 'falling' concept. (This concept cartoon has three children each with a different view: 'The paper falls slowly because it catches the air'; 'The feather falls slowly because it is light'; 'The paper clip falls slowly because it is small'.) For my special needs children I will have at hand objects described in the cartoon — paper clip, paper, feather. I anticipate, because of their confidence, that they will want to discuss their ideas first. I think I will encourage them to discuss their ideas with partners. We will thrash out ideas. I will need to make clear my role which will be not teaching them or leading them in any way to one answer but more as a chair of the discussion so that everyone can speak.

While Emma is clear that she will not be 'teaching' as such in this lesson, the fact that she states it indicates that it is a departure from the norm. She goes on to reflect that she is likely to find it difficult:

> I expect that I will find it difficult to not lead them to one way of thinking and to try to be as neutral as possible. I expect that they will think paper will fall slowly. I want to see if they can independently link air resistance to surface area.

After the lesson she reflected on it thus:

> I felt pleased that I stuck to my intended agenda. I focused on scientific concepts being a result of human endeavour and born from questions and hypotheses. I

referred to scientists that they were familiar with, like Einstein. The children were really quick and keen to generate their own hypotheses for the concept cartoon. They were reassured when I emphasised how I was more interested in what they thought and not to try and guess for the 'right answer'. The hardest thing I found was playing the chairperson and not the teacher when they discussed their ideas – I did what I feared which is rather than listening to them, I kept trying to teach them 'the science' of the lesson and move them to one way of thinking. They were not clear whether weight or surface area was the key factor and some chose the feather and others the paper.

Although it is clear from the above that Emma was adopting a somewhat unfamiliar role in this lesson, the fact that she raises these issues so explicitly and the ways in which she talks about them suggests that she has a clear understanding of the implications in terms of children's learning and engagement, of the way in which she behaves and the roles she adopts in lessons.

Both Becky and Emma found that the experience of opening up discussion around clearly focused activities started to allow children to appreciate aspects of the nature of science and, importantly, become more confident with questioning and discussion:

I think they are more confident in science. They've learned a lot more vocabulary, like, for example, hypothesis and prediction. I would write this word up on the board and might even say 'What is the difference between a prediction and a hypothesis?' and get them to argue about it. They are more confident in working independently. You know, things like the concept cartoons. We hadn't used concept cartoons before the project. And now I can throw a concept cartoon at them and they know what's expected of them. Yeah, working independently and discussion in a group. So it's a way of learning, a style of teaching, that they'd taken on board. They got used to that because we'd done it many times, so they were more confident and … rather than you always having to say Why? they actually say 'because we think blah, blah, blah'. So they got into the habit of trying to make it as full as possible and to always give some kind of explanation. (Becky)

This development of questioning and ability to tolerate different positions on scientific evidence was also apparent in the classrooms of secondary teachers. This research focusing on teachers' practice has helped indicate the nature of professional development that is important in developing effective teaching of the nature of science. In order to realise aspirations for children to really make sense of their world, ask questions, compose and evaluate arguments, teachers should be helped to engage children in dialogue which genuinely questions scientific evidence (i.e. focuses on 'how do we know?' rather than 'what do we know?').

Pause for thought

Teaching the nature of science

Where do you think you lie on the five nature of science dimensions in Figure 1.2? Can you engage children in open-ended discussion? Can you use activities to focus on the 'how we know' as well as the 'what we know'?

Nature of science:

a summary of key points

This chapter has attempted to show the importance of the nature of science in children's education and some of the research evidence available has been highlighted. Yet much remains to be explored. We still do not know enough about progression in the development of children's ideas about the nature of science when it is explicitly taught and large-scale formal assessment of the nature of science is in its infancy. The nature, processes and practices of science are becoming increasingly important in science curricula worldwide and we can anticipate that the nature of science will continue to be the focus of a research and development agenda for many years to come.

JOAN PARKER

Introduction

Securing children's learning in science involves teachers in helping them to develop not only a knowledge and understanding of scientific concepts and explanations but also the skills of scientific enquiry that lie at the heart of science as an enterprise. This chapter focuses on the nature of such knowledge and understanding and what this means in terms of how primary children construct their own ideas. In exploring learning in science, the discussion highlights the role of enquiry skills within the learning process.

What do we mean by knowledge and understanding?

The National Curriculum for primary science (DfEE/QCA, 1999) stipulates that children should acquire the appropriate knowledge and understanding that underpin key ideas about *life processes and living things* (Sc2), *materials and their properties* (Sc3) and *physical processes* (Sc4). While there is no clear differentiation between knowledge and understanding, progression in learning is implied in the shift from *knowing and describing* at Key Stage 1 (Levels 1 and 2) to *describing and explaining* at Key Stage 2 (Levels 3 to 5). This shift in emphasis from describing (or 'knowing that') to explaining (or 'knowing why') suggests that an important aim in primary science education is that children should develop coherent and meaningful representations of the scientific ideas they engage with. However we attempt to define knowledge and understanding, they are fundamentally cognitive processes in which learners synthesise a range of experiences in order to make sense of science at a level appropriate to their development (for further discussion see Newton, 2001). Significant differences in levels of insight need to be defined if claims are to be made regarding the levels of knowledge and understanding demonstrated by a learner. In forces, for example, there is a spectrum of possible uses of the word 'force' ranging from the tactile experiences associated with pushes and pulls to the highly abstract reasoning involving weight as the gravitational attraction between an object and the Earth. Children also encounter the word 'force' in everyday contexts outside school (e.g. the police force, 'may the force be with you', and so on).

Pause for thought

Knowledge, understanding and generating causal mechanisms

A common feature of developing knowledge and understanding in science is the need for learners to develop qualitative insight such that the ideas being engaged with make sense (i.e. they generate a causal mechanism to explain a phenomenon). Consider your own views on the following commentary associated with learning about shadows and shadow formation. In the useful summaries provided by

Osborne et al. *(1990) and Driver* et al. *(1994a), it has been noted that children tend to think of a shadow in terms of the presence of an object or a person that light allows them to see rather than the absence of light itself. Shadows are also thought of as entities with their own properties, hiding in objects or people until pushed away from them. While shadows are often known to reproduce an object's or a person's shape or general form, explanations of predictions often confuse the word shadow with reflection (as in the outline of an object or a person in a mirror). Children usually fail to notice the relationship between shadows and the passage of light in straight lines.*

- *To what extent do your own ideas match those of children?*
- *How do teachers become effective at promoting 'knowing why' as opposed to just 'knowing that'?*
- *Is there too much privileging of knowledge at the expense of understanding in the science curriculum?*

How are knowledge and understanding acquired?

The view that scientific knowledge cannot be transmitted easily or directly from one individual to another continues to underpin contemporary perspectives on science education today (Driver *et al.*, 1994b). Indeed, research has demonstrated the fundamental importance of children's own ideas in the learning of science and the need for classroom practices that respond to them in appropriate ways. This requires of the teacher a range of strategies to support learning and recognition that particular conceptual areas require particular pedagogical expertise. The following discussion explores some implications of approaches towards the teaching and learning of science both through an historical perspective and directly through examples of children learning.

Approaches towards teaching science in the primary school

A key question in science pedagogy concerns how teaching can effectively support children in acquiring their knowledge and developing understanding. Addressing this problem has had significant influence in the way in which science has been approached in the primary school.

Science as enquiry

Historically, there has been particular emphasis on the importance of practical work in primary science education. Scientific enquiry in the National Curriculum constitutes an investigative approach to developing scientific explanation and forms the most significant single element of the Programmes of Study. The value of this resides in the notion that providing children with opportunities to test their own ideas alongside scientific explanations enables them to develop a rationale for making sense of the world around them. This idealist position is rooted in the conceptualisation of the child as scientist and from this evolved an approach to science teaching based on discovery methods of learning. Prior to the implementation of the National Curriculum in primary schools, the guiding principle for effective science teaching was concerned with children *doing* science, with the *learning* of science as a body of knowledge and explanation very much a secondary consideration. However, as pointed out by Hodson (1998), discovery by *doing* often assumed that children who were engaged in science activities at school and constructing their own knowledge and understanding of the world around them were also constructing scientific knowledge and understanding of the world around them, and that anything was allowed to count as science provided that children were working cooperatively and in a friendly learning environment. Thus by engaging in practical investigations and enquiries, all children were considered scientists. As Hodson explains, not all investigations and enquiries are scientific and not all forms of knowledge and understanding arising from them are equally valid from a scientific point of view. The debate on what would make for appropriate content, raised by Harlen (1978), and indeed whether a specified content was necessary in the primary school, was largely succeeded a decade later when the National Curriculum specified the knowledge and understanding required of children at Key Stages I and 2.

From process to product

With the National Curriculum came a profound shift in emphasis that challenged the relative balance between the *doing* of science as investigative process and the *learning* of science as a body of knowledge. The legacy of discovery learning is evidenced in the nature of investigative scientific enquiry that underpins the development of knowledge and understanding. However, with the current curriculum focus on subject knowledge there is the danger that requirements for scientific enquiry will be increasingly conceptualised as experimental procedure focused on controlling variables and fair testing. While there is excellent practical support for this aspect of teaching (e.g. Goldsworthy and Feasey, 1997), the narrowing of the intended experience of scientific enquiry may lead to a closing down of discourse in teaching and learning. This has the effect of perpetuating the notion that teaching and learning in science is essentially about knowledge acquisition. The recent introduction of national tests (still widely referred to as Standard Assessment Tasks or SATs) for scientific enquiry at Key Stage 2 may go some way in addressing this issue. However, until scientific enquiry is truly viewed as an integral part of learning science, the narrowing of this intended experience is likely to continue.

Pause for thought

The role of practical work in primary science

Leach and Scott (2003) argue that the practical based approaches to teaching and learning science currently prevalent in primary schools represent a view of 'active' learning that has become the norm:

> *We believe that these approaches are based on an underlying view of science learning as a process whereby individuals change their ideas in response to*

(mainly perceptual) information. What is missing in the areas of research and teaching is any real recognition of the central role of the teacher in introducing science ideas to the classroom and controlling the 'flow of discourse'. The ability to guide the classroom discourse as ideas are explored and explanations are introduced is central to the science teacher's skill and is critical in influencing students' learning. This argument should not be taken as a stance against practical work. Rather, we are arguing that in most cases practical work should be concluded in such a way that the main part is for students to interact with ideas, as much as the phenomena themselves.

If teachers are to 'control the flow of discourse' and engage students in interaction with ideas, what are the implications for:

- *teacher subject knowledge and pedagogical content knowledge?*
- *the role of investigative work in developing conceptual understanding?*
- *the range of science activities provided?*
- *the breadth and depth of the primary science curriculum?*
- *creative approaches to science?*

Constructivism in science education and the importance of children's ideas

The resolution of addressing how to make scientific ideas accessible to children at an appropriate level has been a driving force behind the constructivist movement in science education. While the term constructivism is multifaceted and much debated (e.g. Solomon, 1994; Fox, 2001), it encompasses a wide range of influences in both research and teaching and has had a pervasive influence throughout the primary age phase. Presented in various ways in the literature, constructivism essentially portrays a view of learning in which each child constructs his or her own knowledge as he or she interacts with the objects, events and phenomena of science within a range of personal and social contexts. Although there is no specific emergent teaching metho-dology arising from such a view of learning (e.g. Millar, 1989), constructivist approaches towards teaching and learning science are necessarily concerned with children's ideas and their development and seek to provide experiences within which learners can sensibly interpret their observations and findings. Teaching, therefore, seeks to foster engagement with ideas and explanations in a process of interpretation and construction and, in doing so, draws on a wide range of approaches.

A significant body of research has emerged which focuses on eliciting children's ideas in science usually before any formal instruction takes place at school and this has provided useful insights into what learners know and how they think across a wide range of conceptual domains (Duit, 2003). Variously described as *preconceptions*, *misconceptions* and *alternative interpretational frameworks*, the literature tells us that children's ideas about science are often incommensurate with scientific explanation and that these ideas are significant in the learning process. This is hardly surprising as many scientific explanations are counter-intuitive, non-spontaneous and often based upon abstract reasoning. Children's ideas can also be robust and resistant to change, thereby presenting a significant challenge in the quest for effective science teaching. So how does constructivism manifests itself in classroom practice?

The practical application of constructivism to the crucible of the classroom is a precarious activity (Solomon, 1994) but was the basis for at least two major research initiatives in the 1980s and 1990s aimed at developing instructional strategies informed by evidence. The Children's Learning in Science project (CLIS 1988–1992) and the primary Science Processes and Concept Exploration project (SPACE 1990–1998) focused on the elicitation of children's ideas about scientific phenomena. These projects highlighted the extent to which children agreed with scientifically accepted views within a wide range of conceptual domains or not and the extent to which their ideas could be changed. The primary SPACE research spawned the Nuffield Primary Science Teachers' Guides (1995) that constituted a new approach to science education. These provided a variety of elicitation strategies appropriate for the primary classroom (including questioning, writing down ideas, developing annotated drawings, sorting and classifying, and using log books and diaries in order to record changes over longer periods of time) and employed teaching strategies designed to develop children's thinking:

- **letting children test their own ideas;**
- **encouraging generalisation from one context to another;**
- **discussing the words children use to describe their ideas;**
- **extending the range of evidence available to children;**
- **getting children to communicate their ideas.**

Concept mapping used in science can also provide insight into how children associate experience and ideas and how these are related to each other. It involves children associating selected concepts, drawing arrows between concepts to show how they are related and then describing the relationship (for further details see White and Gunstone, 1992; Sharp *et al*, 2002).

Developing children's knowledge and understanding in practice

As we have seen, a constructivist view of learning based on developing children's ideas about scientific phenomena is now widely accepted in science education. Children of all ages possess preconceived ideas about every scientific area taught in the curriculum and these ideas are integral to the teaching and learning process. From the work of Driver and Bell (1986):

- **children make sense of the world around them on a personal level which is rooted in past experience and direct observation;**
- **children necessarily build upon their limited past experiences and there is no guarantee that what they learn will reflect anything scientific;**
- **children's ideas can be strongly held and resistant to change;**
- **children's ideas are context specific.**

How then might learning, the changing of these intuitive ideas into appropriate scientific explanations, take place? Harlen (1992b) presents a model of learning based on evidence drawn from observing children and adults making sense of new happenings as well as reflecting on how scientists try to explain new observations. She contends that when children are faced with something new they search around, often unconsciously, and use previous experience in trying to understand it. They link previous experience to the new object or events. For example, in a study of Year 5 children exploring the properties of paper, children were given the opportunity to look closely at paper for the first time using strong magnifying glasses (Parker, 1995). They made some interesting associations, noting that it looked like '… hare (hair)', '… wool in a mess', '… a carpet' and '… cotton wool'. Here, the children are seeking to connect their new experience with something familiar; they are associating the structure of paper with other structures they have encountered before. Indeed, we often deliberately try to harness the same process in science teaching when we use analogies and metaphors to help learners make sense of abstract scientific notions. However, because children have more limited life experience than adults, they have less to choose from in making linkages.

In Harlen's model, once an idea has been linked, its usefulness in explaining the situation has to be tested. If the results of this testing are to be useful in promoting understanding then the testing must be rigorous. Testing may simply involve further observation (e.g. the child who doesn't know how plants grow needs to watch the germination of seeds) or a focused investigation (e.g. the child who thinks that the Sun and the Moon are two halves of the same astronomical body that rotates to cause day and night needs to see both objects in the sky at the same time, to record their apparent movements, and to consider different possible interpretations). The outcome of testing is that an idea is confirmed, strengthened or changed in some way. Change may involve modifying the idea to fit with evidence or rejecting it altogether and adopting an alternative. However, young children are unlikely to possess well developed testing skills and will need to be supported and guided in acquiring them during their primary education. Also, as children have limited experiences and fewer concepts with which to link, then a key role of primary education is to extend and broaden their interactions within the physical, material and biological worlds.

Harlen thinks that ideas that are not linked to previous experience are of little use in explaining new experience and are committed to memory by rote or restricted to the contexts in which they are developed. Similarly, Watt (1998) refers to learners having a 'mental store' in which ideas and experiences are organised so that similar ones are grouped together making a general definition of the topic or experience. Children of all ages, for example, often reveal a strong association between 'electricity' and 'making' things happen (Figure 2.1). Watt contends that broad organising groups or concepts are an essential part of developing understanding and if we are to help children to make sense of their world then we must help them to create this order so they can use specific information with meaning. Without such linkage we have unrelated pieces of knowledge that are of limited use.

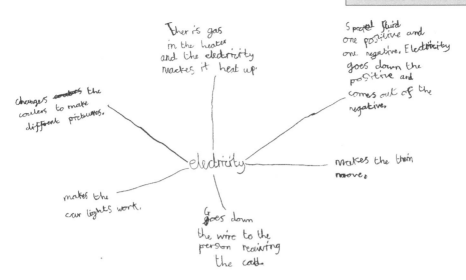

Figure 2.1. Child's associations with regard to electricity (aged 7 years)

Electricity

Electricity provides some of the best examples of children's alternative and scientific ideas in science and highlights the subject knowledge and pedagogical demands placed upon primary teachers themselves. At Key Stage 2, teaching about electricity is concerned with building simple circuits incorporating a battery or power supply and a range of switches to make simple electrical devices work. Children are taught how to change the number of components or their type in a series circuit to make bulbs glow brighter or dimmer and how to represent and construct circuits using drawings and conventional symbols. Essentially, these requirements are technological and do not concern any scientific explanation of electricity and its manifestations. And yet research has shown that children are guided by their reasoning about electricity and how it behaves (Driver et al., 1985). Being able to construct simple circuits is dependent upon having an underlying conception of a complete circuit that entails knowledge of connection points on both battery and components. Parker and Heywood (1996) found that despite prior experience of circuit building, few 8- and 9-year-old children in their study had internalised the concept of a complete circuit. The study explored children's reasoning underpinning the practical activity of circuit building and found four categories of initial thinking (Figure 2.2). Similar categories have also been found elsewhere (Osborne and Freyberg, 1985; Shipstone, 1985).

The sink model is confirmed by lots of life experiences where materials are stored in containers and then used up (e.g. pouring liquid out of bottles, batteries going flat). The notion of two wires being better than one is widely confirmed in life experience. As one child remarked: 'it's like if you use two straws to drink your milk'. A clashing current model is suggestive of an electrical shock (children are taught about the dangers of electricity at Key Stage 1) or possibly high speed collisions or reactions that emit light (a situation often portrayed in children's media). Correct electrical connections were rare:

To make the bulb light up you need a complete circuit. You need to put the wires on the top and bottom of the battery and side and bottom of the bulb.

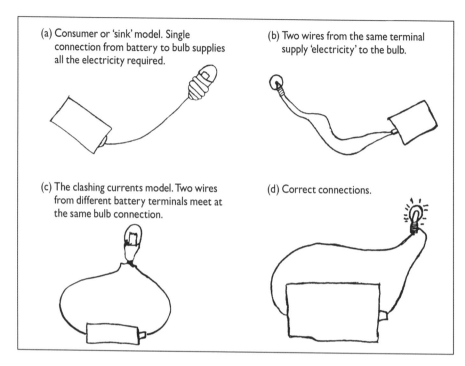

(a) Consumer or 'sink' model. Single connection from battery to bulb supplies all the electricity required.

(b) Two wires from the same terminal supply 'electricity' to the bulb.

(c) The clashing currents model. Two wires from different battery terminals meet at the same bulb connection.

(d) Correct connections.

Figure 2.2. Children's ideas about how to light a bulb

Interestingly, even when correct electrical connections are made, children may still think that electricity flows out of either end of the battery and clashes at the bulb or that as electricity flows through the bulb, current is consumed. Thus, in building circuits children are guided by their underlying conceptions and there is evidence in their reasoning of linking ideas with past experiences.

Children's underlying conceptions are powerful in guiding their reasoning when making predictions about the behaviour of a host of possible circuits. Effective teaching cannot escape engaging with ideas and teaching needs to help children to interpret abstract and difficult notions and build understanding at an appropriate level (for further details read more about electricity later in this book).

Other examples

Of course, children's ideas are not unique to electricity. Research findings from nursery to Year 6 confirm that children appear to grow up with a limited knowledge and understanding of what plants are, the factors responsible for their growth, how they reproduce, and the diversity of plants within the plant kingdom as a whole. Stereotypical images of plants as simply 'flowers' persist until well beyond the primary years. In two early studies by Bell (1981) and Bell and Barker (1982), only about 25% of the 7-year-olds and 60% of the 11-year-olds involved considered humans to be animals and worms and spiders were only considered to be animals by 30% of both age groups. The concepts of 'plant' and 'animal' clearly require some attention and careful development. In a study by Russell and Watt (1990), children were asked what went on inside a hen's egg during incubation. Most thought that there was a miniature hen in the egg that simply got bigger by expanding in size (Figure 2.3). A few children even believed that the egg contained an assemblage of individual body parts that came together over time. Only a small number believed in the actual transformation of the egg's contents.

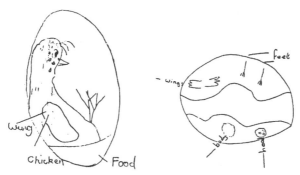

Figure 2.3. How living things grow (from Russell and Watt, 1990)

When sorting and classifying materials, young children tend to choose criteria on the basis of tactile experience (e.g. whether or not they can be bent). As they get older they tend to use more complex criteria such as function (e.g. building materials). Solids are often thought of as hard, can be held or touched and heavier than liquids but the range of solids can be too diverse for the purposes of generalisation. Liquids, on the other hand, can be poured and they run. The 'runniness' of some fine-particle solids can lead to confusion. Children also tend to compare liquids in terms of how much like water they are. Gases are more difficult. Air is usually only ever considered to be a single gas rather than a mixture and often used synonymously with oxygen. Sprays, mists, smoke and flames are also regarded as gases. Understanding what happens during changes of state, dissolving and chemical reactions is difficult.

When describing forces, many children often ascribe animal or human attributes to inanimate objects in order to explain what happens. Such animistic and anthropomorphic thoughts are common throughout science. Forces are also commonly thought of as having an obvious effect (e.g. making something move rather than remaining stationary) or as being contained within a moving object and disappearing when it stops. According to Osborne et al. (1990), light is also problematic. Light may just exist rather than travel from one place to another and the Moon is often considered a primary source of light like the Sun. Vision is readily perceived as an active process in which 'rays' are emitted from the eyes (Figure 2.4). This 'looking daggers' model may come from the fact that in order to see an object heads must be turned and eyes focused or that we stare or 'cast' a glance across a room. The 'X-ray' vision seen in comic books and cartoons does not help.

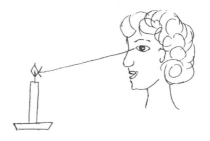

Figure 2.4. How we see (from Osborne *et al.*, 1990)

Similarly with sound, children often associate what they hear with a physical action but may not be aware of anything vibrating. According to Watt and Russell (1990), this is even true when watching the action of moving rice scattered across the skin of a drum (Figure 2.5).

Figure 2.5. How sounds are made (from Watt and Russell, 1990)

Astronomy is also particularly interesting. Studies indicate, for example, that many children start school with ideas about the shape of the Earth that are anything but scientific. Some believe that the Earth is flat, some think it hollow and covered with a dome-like sky, and some think that there are two Earths, the one they live on and the one they hear about in class (Figure 2.6).

Figure 2.6. A dual-Earth model

Some factors influencing the learning process

The socio-cultural dimension

Cognitive science has evolved a view of learning situated within the mental structure and functioning of individuals' minds. As Leach and Scott (2003) reflect, although children's *alternative interpretational frameworks* have been described variously in the literature (e.g. preconceptions, misconceptions and the intuitive and transitional mental models of Vosniadou, 1994), they are not necessarily, in themselves, enough to explain how students learn science *in classrooms*. The socio-cultural perspective provides a major challenge to the tradition of mental structures as it represents a view of learning derived from social interaction (Vygotsky, 1978; Wertsch, 1991). In the social sphere, language provides the means by which individuals explore ideas. Internalisation as a result of social interaction is a process whereby individuals develop and become able to use tools, physical and conceptual, as well discursive, within the social context. Conceptual change, therefore, is perceived not only as an individual process but also as the result of interaction between the learner, tools and other people. The nature of the socio-cultural environment and the extent to which it encourages discussion of and engagement with personal and scientific ideas is important in learning science.

Language and learning in science

Scientific social language, the scientific way of talking and thinking, represents a different way of communicating than in everyday life. Learners' conceptions, however, represent communication in everyday social language and a goal of science teaching, therefore, is to introduce a new way of thinking and talking to children and illustrating and modelling how this is used in particular situations. A radical position to subscribe to would be to consider science teaching and learning to be less concerned with physical phenomena and more concerned with the words that we use to describe them and the stories and metaphors that surround them in building understanding. Indeed, Watts and Bentley (1994) have even gone as far as suggesting using children's own animistic and anthropomorphic thoughts and other figurative language for its pedagogical value in an effort to better 'humanise' and 'feminise' the science curriculum (to make it more 'user' friendly).

The English language is rich in descriptive words and one of the aims of literacy education is to extend and broaden children's knowledge and use of vocabulary. However, when it comes to the specific use of words in science, problems of interpretation and communication can arise. For example, learning about materials and their properties invariably entails teachers and children in description and here language is paramount. This is exemplified by returning to the study of children learning about paper (Parker, 1995). It demonstrates how systematic use of children's descriptive words can help to link their ideas. It was intended that the children investigate the strength of different types of paper; however, it soon became obvious that *strong* and *weak* were terms rarely employed by the children in describing paper and consequently such an activity was likely to prove relatively meaningless. In order to establish a link between paper and the notion of strength it was necessary to focus on the meaning of words and through practical experience to enable the children to expand their concept of the property of *strength*. Initial description of a range of papers revealed that:

- **the most frequently employed descriptive terms were *rough, smooth, thick, thin, heavy, light, soft, hard*;**
- **children sometimes used the same word to describe different things and different words to describe the same thing (e.g. *hard* and *thick*);**
- **children very rarely used *strong* or *weak* in the context of paper although they did recognise them as opposites.**

The children's language was likely to be context-specific. *Strong* things were associated with objects that were heavy or difficult to break whereas *weak* things were the opposite of this. Also *strong* and *weak* were often associated with living things, (e.g. weightlifter, elephant, fly). This carried an affective quality in that being *strong* was generally seen as a good thing and being *weak* was undesirable. Consideration of what they meant by these terms resulted in the children realising that the terms were only meaningful if used comparatively. There emerged a common view that *strength* related to how easily a material could be broken. Using this definition the children carried out a systematic investigation of the strengths of a range of papers and the results revealed that some were surprisingly strong. For many children this constituted a discrepant event in learning, being contrary to their expectations, and was an opportunity to encourage the generalisation of the concept. Observation using magnification prompted discussion of layers, holes and even the relative sizes and arrangements of fibres thereby helping children to explain their observations meaningfully:

> I think that the brown paper was stronger than the kitchen roll because fibres in the kitchen roll has tiny fibres and the brown paper has more spread out fibres and it has holes.

Again, while statutory requirements seem to require that children know that materials have such properties and have some experience in exploring, teaching necessarily engages with explanation with close observation of language emerging as an essential part of the process. If, as Sutton (1992) argues, words are interpretive instruments of understanding, then effective teaching must engage with their use as children learn science in the classroom.

Instructional analogy

In recent years, primary science has seen a move towards helping children to make sense of challenging abstract notions through the use of instructional analogies. Solomon (1986) has reported that the use of simile and metaphor as well as other forms of productive comparison can be an essential part of children learning science, helping them to clarify their thoughts and ideas particularly when working in unfamiliar territory. The aim of analogy is to encourage learners to take elements from a situation that they have experience and knowledge of (the base domain) and to transfer those attributes to the new situation they are trying to understand (the target domain). Of course the success or otherwise of any instructional analogy depends on the extent to which the experience of the learner resonates with the analogy employed and the extent to which they successfully transfer appropriate elements of the analogy. Physical or other concrete representations are perhaps the most suitable for primary children as they serve to capture and focus attention in a stimulating way encouraging the identification of critical similarities and differences. As Asoko and de Bóo (2001) recognise, all analogies have limitations and are useful for transferring only certain elements of a situation. That is, they can be productive or unproductive. Indeed, analogies can provide scope for building misconceptions that may well prove to be an obstacle to learning at a later date. According to Dagher (1994), for example, meaningful learning via the use of instructional analogy is not so much a function of whether an analogy is actually used as much as it is a function of how it is used, by whom, with whom and how it is evaluated. While productive comparisons undoubt-edly help some children to clarify their thoughts, the effectiveness of such approaches as a pedagogical device remains to be fully explored.

Attitudes towards learning in science

It has long been known that attitudes towards science constitute an important affec-tive element in learning and that a range of attitudes may impact upon an individual's motivation to engage with it (Hodson, 1998). Past experiences of learning in science are highly influential, especially when individuals perceive themselves as having failed at science and find it difficult to accept and understand the explanations that science has to offer (Parker and Spink, 1997):

> For me, the definition of science was purely physics and chemistry, both of which I found incredibly difficult and had many negative experiences with. My general ideas of physics and chemistry were scientific symbols and impossible equations, which I failed to solve, however hard I tried.

If such attitudes are to be avoided in primary classrooms, teachers must find ways of promoting science in a more positive light, ways predicated on developing interest, curiosity, enjoyment, enthusiasm and a sense of satisfaction in addition to acquiring knowledge and understanding.

Pause for thought

The construction of scientific knowledge in the classroom

Considering the various positions concerning the acquisition and development of knowledge and understanding presented throughout this chapter, and drawing on your own experiences of studying and teaching primary science so far, imagine how you might you go about challenging the following statements:

- *the bones in your hand are soft and bendy ... that's how you can grab stuff;*
- *the beans will germinate in the sunshine ... it's called photosynthesis;*
- *when you add the sugar to the tea it melts ... it melts more when it's hotter;*
- *I need another red wire to make the bulb light, the black one won't work.*

- *The Sun is a primary source of light ... it's like oil burning.*
- *Gravity's like a magnet ... it pulls you down.*

Can you identify the errors and misconceptions? Which teaching strategies and other pedagogical devices might you use? Which resources would you select? How might you reinforce and extend any learning that takes place?

Knowledge and understanding:
a summary of key points

While there is no set prescription for helping children to acquire knowledge and understanding effectively in science there is a range of practices that support learning in different contexts. These include providing the opportunity for children to test their ideas and where possible to have tactile and other experiences that they can refer to in developing their ideas further. Research in science education under the broad umbrella of constructivism has provided a significant insight into children's ideas across a wide range of phenomena and this is a useful foundation from which to proceed in developing a range of approaches to teaching. While constructivist approaches to teaching have their own disadvantages, it nevertheless reflects good practice in pedagogy and offers a structured approach in which the teacher is aware of the children's conceptual frameworks and an understanding of some of the processes associated with learning itself. The issue of explaining science across a wide subject domain is always going to present a challenge but it is worth referring to an important tenet of constructivism concerning the fact that the construction of meaning is a continuous and active process. Viewing science in this way enables both teacher and learner to feel more confident about their own ideas and the sharing and consideration of these in discourse. This is not the same as saying the teacher does not need to have considered their own knowledge and understanding in terms of how they might coherently explain scientific explanations that are encountered in the learning of science. It is certainly not useful to simply state that the ideas of science are difficult and then to look for a means of escape. A more productive way of looking at the problem is to explicitly recognise that the construction of meaning as a continuous and active process applies equally to the teacher as it does to children. Developing an appropriate curricular expertise in science affects everyone from the most inexperienced to those who would claim to know it all.

3 ACQUIRING SCIENTIFIC SKILLS
ANNE GOLDSWORTHY

Introduction

Ask primary teachers to tell you what they think is important in science education and they are far more likely to respond that it is to do with practical skills such as finding out, asking questions, collecting data or considering evidence than with an accumulation of knowledge about the human body, materials or forces. While everyone now agrees that science education is actually about both knowledge and skills, and that the content of science cannot be developed through practical work alone, teachers know that scientific enquiry is a very important part of a child's scientific education. However, they are far less sure about how to teach it.

Many teachers come to practical work in science with their own expectations about what it should be like from their own school days when a good deal of their practical work was about confirming knowledge. Experiments were almost always carried out with the aim of 'proving' a known fact. Good demonstrations that illustrate a piece of knowledge are useful but they should not be confused with work that helps children come to an awareness of the nature of evidence and that lets them make decisions about how to collect evidence and what it tells us. Of course, helping children towards reliable scientific knowledge by way of collecting and interpreting evidence, and the skills required to do so, demands considerable expertise on the part of the teacher. This chapter draws on the findings of the AKSIS (Association for Science Education and King's College Science Investigations in Schools) project in order to look at the skills children need to deal with scientific evidence and how they can be best helped to acquire and apply these skills.

What do we mean by scientific skills?

There are many classroom activities in which children use equipment and carry out practical tasks but in only some of these activities will children actually use scientific skills. If you want to show your class how something works, for example, you could get equipment out from the cupboard, give your children clear instructions about what to do, and tell them what the activity shows. You may well let them all handle equipment and carry out a practical activity that effectively illustrates and confirms a piece of scientific knowledge, but you would not necessarily have given your children a chance to use or develop their scientific skills. They would not have raised their own questions, planned what to do to get evidence, predicted what might happen, collected evidence through measurement and systematic observation, presented the information in tables, charts and graphs, interpreted the evidence and discussed the strength of the evidence itself.

Although there is broad agreement about what scientific skills are, there is, nevertheless, some variation. Goldsworthy and Feasey (1997) and Harlen (2000) suggest that scientific skills include raising questions, developing hypotheses, predicting, planning, gathering evidence (including making observations, comparisons and measurements), fair testing, interpreting and drawing conclusions, communicating (including constructing and using tables, charts and graphs and explaining results) and reflecting or evaluating. Many other authors offer similar lists. The Programmes of Study for Key Stages 1 and 2 within the National Science Curriculum (DfEE/QCA, 1999) puts investigative skills under three main headings: planning, observing and presenting evidence, and considering evidence and evaluating. In more detail:

- **children should consider what sources of information, including first-hand experience and a range of sources, they will use to answer questions;**
- **children should use simple equipment and materials appropriately and take action to control risks.**

What all lists of skills have in common is that they focus on all those things children do to collect and make sense of evidence. It is not always the activity itself but what children do within it that is important. If, for example, you wanted to demonstrate the properties of gases, you might give each group two balloons, tell them to inflate one and ask them to compare the weights of the deflated and inflated balloons by putting them on a balance bar. You might then explain to the class that because the inflated balloons drop down, they are heavier than the deflated balloons and therefore the gases inside the balloons must have weight. If you worked in this way, you would have taken all the decisions about what to do and what the evidence showed. You would have used some scientific skills but your class would not (other than the simplest comparison of the weight of the two balloons). An alternative approach would be to ask your class whether they think gases have weight or not and to ask them to plan an activity using balloons to help them find out. This will still require considerable guidance from you, the teacher, depending on the previous experience of the children. You would compare results from different groups at the end and discuss what the evidence showed. There may be times when a good demonstration is very useful to illustrate a piece of knowledge but unless the children are involved in taking some decisions about what evidence to collect, how to collect it and what the evidence tells them, they are not developing their use of scientific skills. These skills contribute to the overall understanding of science. Through their application knowledge and understanding will be enhanced.

What do we mean by scientific enquiry?

The title now given to understanding the nature of evidence and the use and application of scientific skills is scientific enquiry. Scientific enquiry should not be confused with the fair test. The fair test, although useful, is only one of many ways of investigating and getting evidence. The AKSIS project looked at the variety of types of enquiry that teachers and children carried out as they taught science in the National Curriculum. About 1,000 teachers from Key Stage 2 and Key Stage 3 were asked to describe the last scientific enquiry they had carried out with their class and responses were classified accordingly (Table 3.1). Categories related to the structure of the investigations rather than any teaching or management issues including whether they were a part or whole investigation, or whether they were individual or group investigations. The different types of enquiry identified were pattern-seeking, exploring, classifying and identifying, making things, fair testing and using and applying models.

I.	Pattern-seeking	2%
2.	Exploring	16%
3.	Classifying/identifying	9%
4.	Making things	12%
5.	Fair test	50%
6.	Using and applying models	0%
7.	Unclassifiable insufficient evidence	5%
8.	No investigation	6%

Table 3.1 The distribution of scientific enquiry types used by teachers in Key Stage 2

Pattern-seeking

Pattern-seeking involves children in looking for trends. If you are trying to find out whether leg length affects the height to which someone can jump, for example, you can't alter their leg length while keeping other factors, such as muscle strength and body mass, the same. Children have to take into account the importance of selecting a suitable sample size in order to account for natural variation. For example, if they want reasonably reliable evidence they should consider whether to ask three people or thirty people before measuring their legs and their jumps.

Investigative questions include:

> *Do people with longer legs jump higher?*
> *Do dandelions in the shade have longer leaves than those in the light?*
> *Where do we find most snails?*

Exploring

Exploring involves children in making careful observations of objects or events, or making a series of observations or measurements of a natural phenomenon occurring over time. They make decisions about exactly what to observe and the number and frequency of observations or measurements.

Investigative questions include:

> *How does frog-spawn develop over time?*
> *What happens to the length of a shadow throughout the day?*
> *How does the temperature of a beaker of hot water change if it is left to cool down?*

Classifying and identifying

Classifying is a process of arranging a large range of objects or events into manageable sets according to their features or the way they behave. Identifying is a process of recognising objects and events as members of particular sets and allocating names to them. Classification and identification both involve children in procedures that discriminate between the things being studied.

Investigative questions include:

How can we group these invertebrates?
Which things are waterproof and which are not?
What is the name of this tree?

Making things

Investigations that involve making things are often technological in nature and involve children in designing an artefact or system to meet a human need. Only those investigations that have a high scientific content, such as knowing that a complete circuit is needed to make an electrical device work, should be considered.

Investigative examples include:

Can you find a way to design a pressure pad switch for a burglar alarm?
How could you make a weighing machine out of elastic bands?

Fair testing

These investigations are concerned with observing and exploring relations between variables or factors. Fair tests involve children in changing one factor and observing or measuring the effect, while keeping other factors the same.

Investigative questions include:

How does the temperature of water affect the time sugar takes to dissolve?
Do different types of paper towel absorb different amounts of water?

Using and applying models

The sixth type of investigation identified by the AKSIS project was that of using and applying models where children develop a theory and devised a model to test it. Such requirements are particularly advanced for children throughout the primary years and examples are perhaps rare.

The AKSIS project, carried out in 1999, showed that there was a heavy emphasis on fair testing with other types of enquiry less well represented. In Key Stage 3 the emphasis on fair testing was even more pronounced. The dominance of fair testing probably occurred because in the early days of Science in the National Curriculum many teachers only received training in this type of enquiry and the line taken was that if practical science didn't involve a fair test it wasn't science enquiry. The AKSIS project found that some teachers encouraged children to apply the fair test structure to activities when it was inappropriate or irrelevant. For example, when children were deciding whether materials were attracted to a magnet or not (a classification enquiry), one teacher asked children how they could make the test fair. The children responded with comments such as 'use the same magnet' or 'have the same person holding it'. In this instance these things are irrelevant. It doesn't matter whether you pick up a different magnet or if another child holds it, the material will either be attracted to a magnet or it won't. This is not a good activity to get at the control of variables (fair testing). If, however, you wanted the children to find out which was the strongest magnet by seeing from how far each magnet could attract a paper clip, then a fair test is essential. You would be changing the type of magnet and measuring the distance from which it attracted the paper clip. Now it is both reasonable and desirable to ask children how they would make this enquiry a fair test and they could respond 'by using the same sized paper clip with each magnet'.

When the AKSIS project team asked teachers what they thought was meant by scientific enquiry, two things dominated. First, that the activity should require children to use scientific skills and procedures. Second, that the children should take some, but not necessarily all, decisions for themselves. They must be given some autonomy at some stage about how the enquiry is carried out and/or how the evidence is interpreted. Teachers may need to guide children to ensure they are not left to reinforce alternative ideas or to draw completely erroneous conclusions.

Pause for thought

What is scientific enquiry?

Teachers in the AKSIS project (1999) said that a scientific enquiry should require children to use scientific skills and procedures and that the children should take some, but not necessarily all, decisions for themselves. How far do you agree with this statement? No classification system is perfect but how well does the classification system described above work for activities carried out in the classroom? Into which category would you put the following?

- *Observing and recording the growth of one bean plant.*
- *Finding out if adults have a different resting pulse rate to children.*
- *Making a filter system to clean dirty water.*
- *Seeing how temperature affects the volume of water that evaporates.*
- *Finding out which materials conduct electricity and which do not.*

Can you think of any primary science activities that do not fit into any of the AKSIS categories? Can you think of any activities or instances where using and applying models might be appropriate?

Developing scientific thinking

Unlike the main content areas of science, not enough is known about the way that children develop their knowledge and understanding of scientific skills. However, the AKSIS project found that teachers who used certain strategies in their lessons were more likely to have successful scientific enquiry lessons. These strategies ranged from allowing children some time for constructive play with phenomena to encouraging children to argue from evidence and to challenge each other's results. However, the two most important strategies were to teach skills explicitly and to make children aware of the skills and procedures they were learning.

How might these strategies look in the classroom? In the following example, a teacher (T) wants to carry out an investigation into how the temperature of water affects the time artificial sweetener takes to dissolve. She also wants the children (C) in her class to understand why it's useful to take repeat readings.

T: In our next enquiry, we're going to think in particular about repeat readings. What I'll be looking for is someone who can tell me three things, why we bother to take repeat readings, suggest why the readings might not always be the same and how they help us decide how much trust we can have in our evidence. Before we do the enquiry we'll look at why we take repeat readings.

The class carries out a quick activity to help children understand why they might want to take repeat readings. The context is measuring the height of the first bounce of a dropped ball (Goldsworthy and Feasey, 1997).

T: I'll drop the ball from this door frame. I'd like you (indicates child) to mark the height of the first bounce on this strip of paper which is fixed to the wall. I'll drop it several times and we'll do the same thing each time. Let's have a look at the marks on the paper. We did the same thing each time. Why do you think that the marks are not all in the same place?
C: Because the ball sometimes went a bit skewy.
C: The ball didn't always bounce on the same bit of surface.
C: It was difficult to see exactly how high the ball bounced.
C: Because the ball doesn't stay still at the top of the bounce so it's hard to mark.
T: If I put this ruler against the strip of paper then we can see that height of the lowest bounce was about 28 cm and the highest bounce was about 44 cm. I'm going to drop the ball once more. Talk together in your pairs. Suggest two heights between 1 cm and 100 cm. The first should be one that you think is quite likely to be the height of the bounce. The second is one that you think is extremely unlikely to be the height of the bounce. (Teacher records their responses.) Most of you thought that it would be very unlikely to bounce to 1cm or 100cm. You also thought it would be most likely to bounce somewhere between 33cm and 38cm. Can I ask you to say how you made that decision?
C: It's where most of them bounced.
C: It probably won't be near that highest mark because it only went that high once.
T: Suppose I'd only dropped the ball and recorded its height just once and it bounced to 39cm. What would you have to say would be the likely result if I did it one more time?

C: 39cm. It's all you've got to go on.

T: So, which do you think gets you nearest to the most likely result – taking one reading or lots of readings?

C: Lots of readings.

T: Do you think you know why we bother to take repeat readings? Turn to your partner/neighbour and see if you agree with each other.

T: Our results for our repeat readings were 35cm, 44cm, 38cm, 28cm, 35cm, 36cm and 33cm. How much trust would you have in repeat readings that were closely clustered, e.g. 35cm, 36cm, 36cm, 35cm, 36cm?

C: Lots of trust.

T: Yes, they would be very reliable results. How much trust would you have in repeat readings that were not closely clustered, e.g. 56cm, 22cm, 33cm, 35cm, 48cm?

C: Very little trust.

T: They wouldn't be very reliable results. How closely clustered were our readings?

C: Only fairly closely clustered.

T: How much trust do you have in our results?

C: Only some trust.

T: Our next enquiry is about how the temperature of water affects the time artificial sweetener takes to dissolve. Take some repeat readings. Be ready to say why your group took repeat readings, how they helped you decide how much trust you have in your evidence and suggest why the readings might not always be the same. You may want to write notes. I'll choose two or three people to tell us their group's ideas. Write up your report on the sheet (Figure 3.1). Most of the plan is already completed as we all did this one the same way. You will need to fill in the table and complete the section about repeat readings.

It is likely that children who had been through a lesson such as this would know that they had been learning how and why to take repeat readings as well as investigating how long sweetener takes to dissolve. We can't always expect children to pick up higher level skills by doing more and more complete investigations. The skills need to be broken down and taught explicitly so that children can understand what the skills are and how to use them in investigations.

We can draw an analogy between the skills of scientific enquiry and a tool kit. When you start DIY you use pretty simple tools to do pretty simple jobs but you gradually build up the number and complexity of the tools in your kit and your ability to use them effectively. So it is with scientific skills. Children should add more and more skills to go in their tool kit as they progress through school. But just as you need an instruction booklet to go with each new tool, so the skills of enquiry need to be taught. However, a set of shiny unused tools is of no use. Just as it is important to use the tools in making something, so skills need to be applied in practical scientific enquiries.

Our fair test enquiry into the time that sweetener takes to dissolve in water at different temperatures.

We will change the temperature of the water.
We will measure the time it takes the sweetener to dissolve.

We will keep these things the same to make it a fair test:
volume of water, number of stirs, mass (amount) of sweetener.

Here is our table of results:

Temperature of water in degrees C	Time for sweetener to dissolve in seconds			
	Ist go	2nd go	3rd go	Average
20				
30				
40				
50				
60				

Why did we bother to take repeat readings?

Give three reasons why you think the readings weren't always the same.

How closely clustered were your repeat readings? How reliable were your results?

What did you find out about the temperature of the water and the time that sweetener takes to dissolve?

Figure 3.1. Sheet for recording an enquiry about dissolving sweetener with repeat readings

Work from the AKSIS project indicates that this way of teaching skills is effective. How some Year 4 children fared in a pre- and post-test looking at the skill of creating and using bar charts, and how some Year 6 children fared in creating and using line graphs, is indicated as shown in Tables 3.2 and 3.3. The children were taught about bar charts and line graphs using some of the activities outlined in *Getting to Grips with Graphs* (Goldsworthy et al., 1999a). They then applied their new skills in investigations into the growth of plants in different soils (Year 4 bar charts) and change in mass of a wet sponge due to evaporation (Year 6 line graphs). The children showed considerable improvement in their ability to interpret different values, to extrapolate and interpolate and to explain their decisions. They also used bar charts and line graphs more confidently in their investigations.

Another indication that this kind of approach to the teaching of skills is useful to children was reported in Goldsworthy (2000). This work was designed to see the extent to which in-service training that centred on the need to teach skills explicitly, had an impact on classroom teaching and learning. The project helped over 90% of classes make progress.

Question No.	Description	Pre-test N = 33		Post-test N = 32	
QI	Draw bar chart given table	No attempt	9	No attempt	0
		Table copied	15	Table copied	0
		Other incorrect	9	Other incorrect	9
		Minor faults	0	Minor faults	14
		Correct	0	Correct	9
Q2	Ring errors on incorrectly drawn bar chart	No attempt	22	No attempt	6
		Mixed response (errors + non-errors identified)	9	Mixed response (errors + non-errors identified)	0
		I error identified	2	I error identified	7
		2 errors identified	0	2 errors identified	9
		3 errors identified	0	3 errors identified	8
		4 errors identified	0	4 errors identified	2

Table 3.2. Work on graphs: Year 4 – bar charts

Question No.	Description	Pre-test N = 35		Post-test N = 35	
QI	Draw line graph given table	No attempt	10	No attempt	0
		Major faults	23	Major faults	8
		Minor faults	2	Minor faults	11
		Correct	0	Correct	16
Q2	Ring errors on incorrectly drawn line graph	No attempt	25	No attempt	1
		I error identified	10	I error identified	17
		2 errors identified	0	2 errors identified	13
		3 + errors identified	0	3 + errors identified	4

Table 3.3. Work on graphs: Year 6 – line graphs

Pause for thought

Can explicit teaching of skills allow for creativity?

Teaching skills explicitly helps children increase their understanding of the nature of evidence. If skills are taught explicitly in this way, how far is there a danger that children will lose the chance to find their own spontaneous and creative solutions to scientific problems that they encounter? If children are allowed to come up with creative ideas for enquiry will they encounter all the skills they should meet? How can a balance be struck between explicit teaching of skills and creativity?

Communicating ideas and the language of scientific enquiry

One way to allow for creativity in science is to encourage children to record their enquiries in a variety of ways for different audiences. According to Feasey and Siraj-Blatchford (1998), 'communication is crucial to learning in science, where children need to share ideas, solve problems, collect and challenge information, and it is also one way in which science can be made exciting, by introducing different ways of communicating to a wide range of people both inside and outside the classroom'. In their book, *Communication in Science*, they go on to illustrate a variety of communication ideas, none of them centred round the traditional science report and its formal style. For example, some Year 3 children collected their results from growing seeds and presented them on a seed packet that they designed themselves as instructions for sowing seeds. Some Year 5 children wrote a *Which?* style account of their findings about the insulation properties of different cups and a Year 6 class drew up an advertising poster for a new washing-up liquid. Each class wrote about their work for a specific audience who had visited their class at the start of the investigation: a gardener, a caterer and the school cook in the cases cited above. In all instances, the children could see the purpose of their work. None of them had to write a formal science report simply because 'the teacher told them to'.

Another way to record what happens in scientific enquiries is to make use of floor books. Floor books are large books, usually made of sugar paper, in which the teacher writes and draws, often in large felt tip pen or a big font from the computer, to help children tell the story of the enquiry. Floor books are less effective when the teacher provides all the words simply to explain what happened in the enquiry. They are best when the teacher puts down in speech bubbles the comments made by named individual children as well as his or her own questions and comments. These comments can be recorded while the lesson is in progress. If the teacher is the only adult in the classroom, he or she can make this easier to manage with remarks such as 'Just say that again. I think it's one I want to make a note of so I can write it later on in our floor book'. These remarks have a dual role. They can make children feel that having their comment included in the floor book is high status. They can also give the teacher a few extra precious seconds to note what is said. If another adult, such as a teaching assistant, is present they can also note down the comments while the teacher is working with the class.

Floor books work particularly well with younger children in Key Stage 1 who feel that they are unable to write about all that they want to say. Floor books also form a much more effective record of the enquiry, as the richness of what was said in words is not lost when children are asked to write it down. Floor books value children's spoken comments (and the teacher's good questions) and release children from completing reams of worksheets and copying from friends. They also form an attractive display and a useful record of evidence for assessment and monitoring purposes.

Here are some predictions from a Year 2 class that went into their floor book. It was their first enquiry that year and they were investigating what happened to slices of bread when left alone on the table and when wrapped in cling film:

- **The bread that isn't in the cling film might go mouldy. (*Emily*)**
- **The bread on the table might go wet. (*Joe*)**
- **The bread with no cling film might go dry. (*Jordan*)**
- **You won't be able to eat it because it will be all dried up. (*Luke*)**
- **The bread on the table will be all crusty and hard. (*Abigail and Hannah*)**

The floor book went on to record what happened and showed the measurements (length and breadth) of the pieces of bread after three days. The piece in the cling film had shrunk by half a centimetre in each direction while the piece left on the table had shrunk even more. Digital photos also went in the floor book. The final comments were from two children explaining why they thought it had happened:

- **The water had escaped from the one with no cling film. (*Robert*)**
- **The water tried to escape from the one with the cling film but the cling film stopped it. (*James*)**

Floor books can be left in the classroom for children to re-read with their friends. Often they become one of the favourite books in the book corner. The contents are personal and relevant and children tend to talk over the enquiry as they read, putting further emphasis on their oral work. Some schools have taken to recording occasionally in floor books with all age groups, not just the youngest.

Scientific enquiry requires children to use specific types of language and language structures. Children need to speak words in a non-threatening situation to make them part of their vocabulary. Promoting the spoken word is a vital part of developing the language of scientific enquiry. All activities that encourage the language of enquiry and allow children to speak the words they might later use in science are useful. For example, a class of young Key Stage 1 children could play the 'If ... then ...' game which encourages the use of the conditional sentence which they will use later when making predictions and hypotheses in their scientific enquiries. In this game, the teacher puts a collection of small toys, e.g. a penny whistle, a twirling tube and a pop gun, in the centre of a circle of seated children. Children are allowed to try out a toy only when they have said a sentence containing 'If ... then ...'. For example, 'If I pick up this whistle and blow into it then it will make a noise'. Other children take it in turns to say different sentences or repeat ones they have already heard. Whatever happens, the language structure of 'If ... then ...' will become more and more familiar to them. Older children can play a game called *Link the Actions* (Goldsworthy et al., 1999a). In this game two children carry out different actions at the same time. For example, one child could lower their hands slowly while another walks towards the door. The rest of the class thinks up a sentence that says how one action varies with another, e.g. 'The lower the arms the closer to the door' or 'As Jenny's arms got lower so John got closer to the door'.

It is also useful to offer children phrase banks that they might need when discussing their science:

- **To answer our question we needed to …**
- **We decided to change …**
- **We took measurements on the way it affected …**
- **When we looked at the table/bar chart/line graph we saw that …**
- **We thought the graph did that because …**
- **Based on our evidence we think that …**

Older children also need the opportunity to use such phrases in oral discussion and in non-threatening situations before they will feel confident enough to use them in their written work.

Some of the difficulties children encounter with scientific enquiry and ways of addressing them

If you leave children to carry out scientific enquiries on their own, a few will sail straight through, create a good plan and draw reasonable conclusions from their evidence. Many others will meet difficulties along the way. This section looks at three skill areas where children have difficulties and offers ways of helping children under-stand more about the nature of evidence.

Setting up a fair test

When children plan fair tests they can get into difficulties. A Year 5 girl taking part in the AKSIS project wanted to find out how to block sound with different types of material. She placed an alarm clock into various different materials but then got side-tracked into talking about how the different materials affected the pitch of the sound rather than the volume. In another instance some Year 3 children were investi-gating how far cars travelled when released from a ramp. The cars were different colours but otherwise they were similar. Each car was loaded with different weights. The teacher then helped them form the question for investigation 'Which car would travel the furthest?' Children did not appreciate that it was the weight in the car that they were studying rather than the colour of the car. Tom, for example, predicted 'the red car will win the race' indicating that he hadn't recognised that it was the change in weight that mattered, not the change in colour. Asking 'Does the weight in the car make a difference to how far it travels?' would help Tom understand what he was investigating. The teacher also asked children 'What did we keep the same?' and 'Was it a fair test and why?' These questions are really asking the same thing. When the children discussed what they would keep the same, they needed to consider all the things that might make a difference to the distance the car travelled. In this case they needed to mention the height of the ramp, the point of release, the initial force (push) given to the car and, ideally, the car itself. However, the children had difficulty with this. Some of their responses are shown in Table 3.4.

Name	What we kept the same	Was it a fair test?
Tom	Height of the box	Yes – we let the cars go at the same time
Torin	Ramp the same height	Because we didn't change the ramp
Lorna	Pushed the same hardness Ramp kept the same	Started in the same place
Charles	Colour	Started in the same place Let them go without pushing

Table 3.4. Year 2 children's responses to two similar questions about their investigation

One way to help children avoid some of these pitfalls when they set up a fair test is to use what is known as the post-it or sticky label approach. This method is described fully in Goldsworthy and Feasey (1997) and also in Goldsworthy et al. (1999b, 2000). In the instance above, teachers could ask children to respond to the question 'What affects the distance a car can go when released from a ramp?' They might suggest the following:

- **height of ramp;**
- **where we let it go from;**
- **how much of a push we give it;**
- **the type of car;**
- **the weight in the car.**

The children could work in small groups and write each suggestion on a mini-post-it. They could also write what they are measuring – distance travelled – on one more mini-post-it in a different colour. The colour change indicates to the children that this is a different variable type. With support from the teacher as needed, the children set up the fair test by moving the stickers onto a planning board:

We will change
- **the weight in the car.**

We will measure or observe the effect it has on
- **how far the car goes in cm.**

We will keep these things the same
- **height of ramp;**
- **where we let it go from;**
- **how much of a push we give it;**
- **the type of car.**

By swapping one of the stickers from the 'We will keep these things the same' section for the sticker in the 'We will change' slot (e.g. swapping 'weight in car' for 'height of ramp') children can set up alternative fair tests.

Teachers may also encounter younger children who confuse the science meaning of fair (control of variables) with an everyday meaning of fair (fair play). Some young children, for example, were considering how to make jelly dissolve in less time using hotter water. The teacher had prepared jugs of hot, medium and cold water and asked the children how they could make it fair. Every child responded happily that 'it will be fair if we all take turns at stirring' and in an everyday sense they were right. The teacher clarified the meaning for them by asking them to watch while she did the test and to let her know if they spotted her doing anything unfair. She went on to put a large piece of jelly in the beaker of hot water but only a small lump in the beakers of medium and cold water. The children soon informed her that this wasn't fair. She went on to do more stirs in one beaker than the other beakers. Again the children spotted that this also wasn't fair. They went on to carry out the practical work for themselves.

Constructing and using bar charts and line graphs

Children's use of graphs in investigations was also studied as part of the AKSIS project. It was found that most children had difficulty constructing graphs and regarded them as an end in themselves, often drawing conclusions with little or no reference to their graphs at all. Many of the teachers in the AKSIS project recognised that children had difficulties using graphs to describe relationships but few had made a point of teaching them how to go about it or helped them to recognise why it was a useful strategy.

The graph shown in Figure 3.2, taken from Goldsworthy (2000), typifies some of the difficulties encountered. A Year 6 child was investigating how the volume of vinegar affected the amount of gas produced when it was added to a mixture of bicarbonate of soda and water. She timed how long it took the reaction to finish (i.e. for the gas bubbles to stop bursting). The points are plotted correctly but there are no labels on the axes. In conversation, the child did not consider what the pattern on her graph was telling her. She didn't think about what would happen if she added more and more vinegar. As it is, her graph might be taken to indicate that the reaction time would go on increasing for ever. Extrapolate the graph far enough and you could predict that the reaction would never finish even though no extra bicarbonate has been added. In reality, the graph would eventually flatten off but there is no evidence of this, just a simple conclusion that states the more vinegar we add the longer the reaction takes. One way to get children familiar with the idea of describing relationships on graphs is to give them axes based on everyday non-scientific relationships (Figure 3.3).

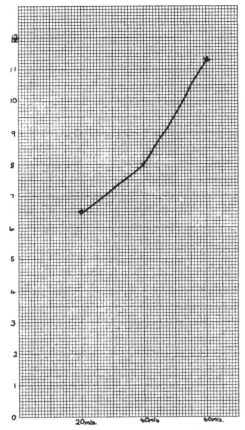

Figure 3.2. Graph from Year 6 child showing how the addition of increasing volumes of vinegar affects the time taken for the reaction of a fixed amount of bicarbonate of soda

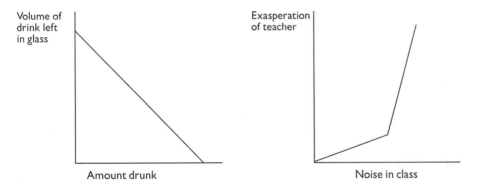

Figure 3.3. Graphs plotted from everyday activities

Children sketch lines on the graphs to show the relationship between the two variables shown on the labels for the axes. It works best when it is used with children as an informal group activity where conversation is encouraged. Most children should draw a straight line in the first example, depicting an inverse relationship. This shows that the more you drink the less is left in your glass. However, you are likely to get several variations on the second graph where children are trying to show how their teacher's exasperation levels vary with the noise in the class. The story that went with the line in the second graph was:

> My teacher is pretty tolerant really if we make a noise while we are working, but that point where the line suddenly gets much steeper – that's when Matthew starts to sing. The noise doesn't increase that much but it sends her exasperation level right up.

If we can encourage children to use line graphs to describe relationships in everyday situations they will have more chance of describing relationships when faced with more scientific graphs.

Drawing conclusions

Many teachers find that it is the end of an enquiry that gets the least attention. Children, like adults, assume that the enquiry stops at the point at which the table is completed or the graph is produced. The AKSIS project found that although teachers planned to spend as much time considering evidence as obtaining it, in reality the time was not allocated equally. Planning and doing often take longer than expected, so children spend far less time considering the evidence. Only a few teachers were able to cite occasions where they had taught children how to draw conclusions or talked about what a good conclusion looked like.

Children often focus on the best performing item in an investigation seeing the enquiry as a competition that will identify a 'winner' (e.g. the best paper towel for mopping up water or the best material for keeping things dry). There is nothing wrong with children finding the 'winner' and for younger children it may be an appropriate response. However, if we want older children to draw a conclusion that says something about all their results, only identifying the best ignores all the other evidence they have collected. This is illustrated in the work from a child in Year 4 who was testing the breaking strength of threads by hanging a bucket from each thread in turn. Increasing weight was added to the bucket until the thread snapped. The child then drew a bar chart (Figure 3.4).

The striking thing about this investigation was that the cotton and nylon seemed to be about eight times stronger than the wool and nylon. This shows up very clearly on the bar chart. Most of us would have predicted a difference in breaking strength but not that two of the threads would be so much stronger. The child doesn't comment on this part of his evidence and simply states that the nylon was the strongest. However, the initial question that started the enquiry was 'Which thread is the strongest?' and he has answered this question. If, instead, the enquiry had asked 'Are all threads the same strength?' this would have encouraged him to look at his other results as well.

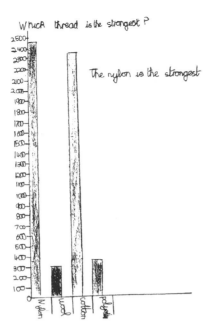

Figure 3.4. Bar chart from a Year 4 child showing the suspended mass needed to break different threads

Acquiring scientific skills:

a summary of key points

For many years, teachers and science educators have wanted children to learn about scientific enquiry. It seems to embody an essential part of what we want them to learn from science lessons and to further their understanding of the nature of scientific evidence. However, there are still aspects of children's understanding of the nature of scientific evidence that are not well understood and current research is just scratching the surface. On their working list, Gott et al. (2003) quote 82 examples of words and concepts that are directly related to scientific enquiry. For teachers to understand all these words and concepts and to help children towards an understanding of them is a very tall order. But there are many things that can be done to help children make progress, some of which have been outlined in this chapter. Teachers can:

- *recognise that there are many different ways to carry out enquiries, not just the fair test;*
- *teach children about the skills and procedures they will need to use in enquiries;*
- *offer a variety of ways for children to communicate their ideas and help them to develop the language associated with scientific enquiry;*
- *appreciate some of the difficulties that children encounter when they use skills and offer some remedies.*

4 CURRICULAR EXPERTISE
DAVE HEYWOOD

Introduction

The expertise required of primary teachers for teaching science in the curriculum has changed dramatically during the last 20 years. This chapter examines the nature of such changing curricular expertise and explores how teachers can develop both subject and pedagogical knowledge in science through a conceptual change-based approach towards learning.

The introduction of a National Curriculum for science (DES/WO, 1989, now DfEE/QCA, 1999) caused national debate about the nature of teacher expertise needed to teach science effectively in the primary school. This resulted in widespread changes in policy relating to the training of teachers. Throughout the 1980s, local education authorities promoted a variety of initiatives aimed at stimulating teachers' interest in science by focusing mainly on developing investigative skills rather than specific scientific knowledge. Science was about exploring and investigating phenomena and developing the skills and attitudes of scientific enquiry. The National Curriculum, however, actually specified what science was to be learnt by children and saw scientific enquiry as the vehicle through which such learning would take place. This placed considerable demands on the primary profession as a whole for several reasons. Few primary teachers at this time were science specialists. Scientific background was likely to be limited and frequently located in the distant past, and teachers often lacked confidence in their own subject knowledge and perceived competence to teach science (Wragg et al., 1989; Carré and Carter, 1990). Subsequently, primary teacher education became a focal point for exploring the development of subject knowledge in science.

Science subject knowledge is an important element of curricular expertise affecting both teachers and trainee teachers alike. Following the introduction of the National Curriculum for science, much of the in-service training of teachers focused on improving teachers' knowledge of science concepts as an integral part of supporting them in implementing the requirements in the classroom. Meanwhile, in initial teacher training (ITT), debate raged about what sort of education would best support trainee teachers within this new framework, and in the same way as the government introduced a National Curriculum for science for all children of compulsory school age, it was somewhat inevitable that changes to ITT would follow. A first attempt to specify a National Curriculum for science in ITT appeared in DfEE Circular 4/98 (DfEE, 1998) which listed the science subject knowledge necessary for intending teachers as well as related pedagogical knowledge and knowledge of effective teaching and assessment. Although it was useful to spell out requirements in one sense, such specification was not without criticism with regard to the appropriateness of the subject matter stipulated and the implicit, yet ill defined, relationship between this subject knowledge and the pedagogical implications of teaching it.

In 2002, Circular 4/98 was succeeded by *The Professional Standards for Qualified Teacher Status for Initial Teacher Training* (DfES/TTA, 2002). Interestingly the science subject knowledge component for primary trainees was no longer stipulated explicitly:

> Central to all teachers' work is the need to help pupils develop their knowledge and understanding of the subjects they study. To do this confidently and effectively teachers need a high level of subject knowledge and understanding relevant to the pupils' curriculum. Secure subject knowledge enables teachers to judge how ideas and concepts can be broken down and sequenced logically so they can support pupils' learning. (TTA, 2002)

The documentation clearly requires not only a sound knowledge of science in the curriculum but also a more subtle knowledge of how this is best translated into effective practice in teaching. It implies that sequencing of ideas and concepts arises from secure subject knowledge and is unproblematic. However, the reality of learning science, especially where the ideas being taught are abstract and counter-intuitive, tells us that this is in fact a complex and individual process.

What do we mean by teachers' curricular expertise?

To begin with we need to consider what we mean by 'curricular expertise'. Primary teachers possess a huge variety of expertise ranging from general pedagogical 'know-how' including managing and organising learning in the classroom for large numbers of children, knowledge of educational goals, values and purposes, knowledge of educational contexts and knowledge of learners themselves. Such types of knowledge transcend individual subjects, being equally important in all aspects of education. In exploring curricular expertise in terms of *science* subject knowledge, however, useful starting points to consider are:

- **teachers' personal knowledge of science (i.e. *substantive* or *content* knowledge of science – the facts, theories, concepts and explanations of science and how they are organised);**
- **teachers' knowledge of how the content of science is generated through scientific enquiry (i.e. *syntactical* knowledge – the processes of science).**

Surveys of both teachers' and trainees' views on science teaching have shown that they frequently lack confidence both in science subject knowledge and teaching (Carré and Carter, 1990; Harlen and Holroyd, 1997; Parker and Spink, 1997). The Oxford-based Primary School Teachers and Science project (PSTS 1989–93) investigating primary teachers' understanding of science concepts in a variety of science domains showed that they often had a limited knowledge of key scientific ideas. Furthermore, teachers sometimes held similar misconceptions as the children they were teaching (Summers, 1994; Summers and Kruger, 1994).

Efforts to raise standards in teaching and training have been underpinned by the implicit assumption that a strong knowledge base will automatically result in better science teaching. However, there is more to curricular expertise than processing knowledge of the subject: there is the crucial issue of how this knowledge then becomes translated into effective teaching. In this sphere, the work of Shulman and his associates (Shulman, 1986) has been highly influential. Shulman makes the distinction between personal subject knowledge of science and what he termed the 'pedagogical content knowledge' important in teaching science. Pedagogical content knowledge concerns how subject knowledge is translated in teaching and as such could be considered *the* critical issue in teachers' curricular expertise. Such knowledge covers a host of issues relating to how teachers represent subject matter and a significant element of this concerns the expertise required to offer different explanations appropriate for learners in particular contexts. For example, it is one thing to know that the forces acting on a floating object are in balance (subject knowledge) but teaching this idea to children effectively requires a sophisticated synthesis of subject and pedagogical expertise of a different nature. It includes, for instance, knowledge of:

- **learners' ideas about the subject being taught;**
- **the nature and progression of ideas (how concepts might be built);**
- **how to represent ideas for learners using metaphors, analogies and effective explanations;**
- **specific difficulties learners are likely to encounter in understanding ideas (e.g. language issues, counter-intuitive scientific ideas);**
- **how children learn science (e.g. importance of multisensory experience and practical activity);**
- **strategies that are effective in teaching (e.g. scaffolding learning).**

In teaching science to children, teachers act as interpreters and translators of scientific ideas. While a precise pedagogical prescription is difficult to define, Smith and Neale (1991) proposed a range of expertise required of primary science teachers in this translation process including knowledge of children's conceptions, the usual developmental path along which children are likely to progress in their learning of science concepts and the errors they are likely to make.

Perhaps the most significant change in science education in the past 20 years has been recognition of the importance of children's ideas about scientific phenomena and their role in learning. During the 1980s, research into children's conceptions was gathering pace (Driver *et al.*, 1985) but in reality teachers rarely possessed awareness of children's scientific ideas or their power to interfere with learning. The work of research projects such as the Children's Learning in Science (or CLIS) project (1987) and the primary-focused Science Processes and Concept Exploration (or SPACE) project (1990–1998) did much to identify children's ideas across the range of the science curriculum and to develop strategies to support teachers in helping children to develop their ideas. There now exists a wealth of information worldwide on children's conceptions (Duit, 2003) and effective teaching is currently seen as being concerned with finding ways to influence children's ideas and to turn them into more scientific ones. At the heart of this lies a view of learning as a process of personal construction by individuals as they interact socially within contexts. The so-called constructivist view of learning pervaded teacher education during the 1990s but it is important to recognise that it reflects a broad church of thinking within which debate continues.

What might a constructivist approach to teaching and learning look like? Appleton and Asoko (1996) suggest that a teacher displaying the following elements of practice might be considered to have a constructivist view of learning:

- a prior awareness of, or attempts to find out about, the ideas which children hold and attempts to elicit them;
- clearly defined conceptual goals and an understanding of how learners progress towards them;
- use of teaching strategies that involve challenge to or development of initial ideas and ways of making new ideas accessible to learners;
- provision of opportunities for learners to apply new ideas in a range of contexts;
- creation of a classroom atmosphere that encourages children to put forward and discuss ideas.

The OFSTED Review of Schools in England (1999) acknowledged explicitly that the most effective teaching makes use of discussion and probing questions to encourage pupils to talk through their ideas and so develop understanding. Thus, curriculum expertise needs to encompass much more than the facts, theories and laws of science; it must also address the issues of effective translation of knowledge in teaching. Summers (1994) in discussing the problems of primary teachers' curricular expertise, recognises both subject and pedagogical knowledge as crucial determinants of teaching performance, inferring that teachers who lack subject knowledge will also lack expertise in pedagogy.

Pause for thought

Science pedagogical knowledge and the primary teacher

In discussing the applicability of the work of Shulman and his colleagues to British primary school teachers, Poulson (2001) questions whether simply improving teachers' science subject knowledge will in turn lead to more effective classroom practice, pointing out that other types of knowledge, for example knowledge concerning children's learning and how abstract scientific ideas are developed, are equally as important as sound subject knowledge. Indeed, as Lunn (2002) comments, despite research that seems to indicate that teachers may have severe gaps in their scientific knowledge, evidence suggests that primary teachers in England are achieving good and improving results in science teaching. For instance, there have been successive improvements in the percentage of children attaining the expected Level 4 or above in Key Stage 2 National Tests (or SATs), reaching 86% in 2002. So it seems that knowledge other than content knowledge may be important here and, as Lunn suggests, perhaps the act of teaching science has somehow transcended the subject matter and given teachers confidence by another route. Is it reasonable to expect primary teachers and trainees to be able to achieve high levels of pedagogical knowledge and expertise in their science teaching given the number of disciplines they are required to deliver in the primary classroom? Given the level of demand in terms of science concepts, particularly in Key Stage 2, should we be training specialist teachers of science?

Orientation

Although the discussion of teachers' expertise has so far focused on subject and peda-gogical knowledge, it is important to recognise that other factors also influence the way teachers teach science. Research has shown that an individual's beliefs about the subject, often referred to as a person's 'orientation', are very important. Such beliefs concern personal views of how best to teach science and how learners' learn science as well as views on the nature of science itself. For instance, Smith and Neale (1991) defined several types of orientation:

- *didactic/content mastery* (science is seen as a body of facts and laws);
- *processes* (science is concerned with scientific method and employing the processes of science such as predicting, inferring and fair testing);
- *discovery* (science is viewed as a process of discovery and is therefore mainly concerned concerned with processes and methods);
- *conceptual change* (science as construction and evolution of theories).

Depending on a teacher's view of the nature of science, teachers may prioritise certain approaches such as the development of scientific enquiry skills or development of factual knowledge or development of personal ideas through teaching strategies employed. Personal orientation is very powerful in determining how an individual teacher delivers the science curriculum in his or her own classroom and, moreover, how the teacher influences the building of images of and orientations towards the subject in the minds of learners.

Pause for thought

Exploring orientation

Gamache (2002) proposes that in order to enhance the learning of students in higher education in general they need to be helped to develop a different epistemological view, one in which they see themselves as creators of 'personal knowledge'. Such an approach requires students to become aware of their own learning and how that takes place on an individual level. In science this may involve radical reappraisal of what constitutes 'science' and 'learning in science'. A useful starting point is to consider past experiences of learning science. What did you learn in science (for example, facts, laws, theories, methods and skills, formulae, scientific explanations)? What teaching methods were employed (e.g. discussing ideas and explanations, recording information, working out problems, carrying out investigations, learning how to use equipment, discovering things for yourself)? How do you feel about science as a result and why do you think you feel this way? How do you think your view informs the way you approach teaching science in the classroom?

Teachers' confidence

Early research revealed a lack of both confidence and *perceived* competence to teach science (e.g. Wragg *et al.*, 1989; Carré and Carter, 1990; Summers and Kruger, 1994). In a comprehensive study by Harlen *et al.* (1995) for the Scottish Council of Research in Education into the nature and scale of problems relating to teacher understanding of scientific concepts and ways in which these might be tackled, a range of effects were identified. Where confidence was low teachers indicated that a limited background in science education, perceived inadequacy of training and the ever-widening remit of teachers were important factors. As Harlen and Holroyd (1997) point out, most teachers lacking in confidence employed a variety of 'coping' strategies. These included for instance, compensating for doing less of a low-confidence aspect of science teaching by doing more of a higher-confidence aspect (e.g. stressing process skills at the expense of concentrating on conceptual development), placing heavy reliance on kits, prescriptive text and pupil work cards, emphasising expository teaching and underplaying questioning and discussion, and avoiding all but the simplest of practical work.

It would, therefore, seem reasonable to assume that improving national standards of attainment for science must reflect growing teacher confidence in the teaching of the subject. Jarvis *et al.* (2001) reported in a study of 64 teachers that 81% were confident or very confident in teaching life processes, although only 54% were as confident when it came to physical processes and 42% investigative science or enquiry. Confidence in planning for science was higher than confidence in assessing science and this probably reflects the role of the *Scheme of Work for Science at Key Stages 1 and 2* (DfEE/QCA, 1998) currently widely employed in English primary schools in supporting teachers in planning. Teachers' knowledge of science and their confidence in teaching it to young children has improved (OFSTED, 2001). However, there are still concerns in some respects, specifically in relation to the teaching of physical processes and scientific enquiry. So although teachers' confidence has risen steadily throughout the 1990s, there is still some way to go in developing confidence across the whole science curriculum.

In-service and pre-service teacher education

Effective science teaching is concerned with helping children to develop progressively more generalised and abstract scientific ideas about the world around them. During the 1990s, both in-service and pre-service teacher education focused on the dual purpose of improving teachers' content knowledge and introducing them to strategies to support children in the development of their ideas. An important element of both pre- and in-service teacher education was an introduction to constructivist approaches to learning and teaching science:

> Many developments in the last 20 years have been influenced by constructivist and social constructivist theories of learning. In essence, a constructivist view of learning suggests that learning involves an active process in which each learner is engaged in constructing meanings, whether from physical experiences, dialogue or texts. (Sharp *et al.*, 2002).

However, for many teachers and trainees, constructivist approaches contrast sharply with personal views and beliefs about teaching and learning science and the process of receiving, interpreting and implementing such ideas in practice is not without difficulty (Wildy and Wallace, 1995; Appleton and Asoko, 1996). It appears that the traditional pattern of single-event in-service training is likely to have only limited effect on teachers' practice; this is hardly surprising as we are dealing with changing fundamental beliefs built on a lifetime experience of teaching and learning. It is important that teachers receive support in applying new ideas to the classroom and this requires long-term professional development with the opportunity to reflect on practice and build on developing knowledge and experience. Although improvement has undoubtedly occurred, studies have indicated that in the long term this was often characterised by coexistence of scientific and intuitive views or that understanding was partial or short lived (Summers and Kruger, 1994). The process of developing science subject knowledge is complex and should not be underestimated.

A model of pre- and in-service education in which teachers undergo conceptual change themselves is likely to be more productive in terms of influencing thinking. Through experiencing conceptual change in action, teachers are more likely to become aware of the salient features of the process and be able to incorporate this knowledge into other areas of their teaching (Harlen et al., 1995). Becoming aware of how learning is being influenced as one goes through the learning process requires a high degree of critical reflection on behalf of learners. Learners need to become aware of how their thinking about phenomena is being influenced by the learning experience and how that results in changes to their reasoning. Such critical reflection on learning is not new to teaching. Indeed, teacher education over the past two decades has subscribed widely to the view that successful practice is linked to reflection on experience and professional enquiry (Loughran, 2002). The following discussion illustrates how critical scrutiny of the learning process by learners can lead to the generation of valuable subject and pedagogical knowledge in practice.

Teachers and trainees developing both science subject matter and pedagogy as they learn about forces

The following illustrates important features of a conceptual change approach to learning science as teachers and trainees learn about forces during university taught sessions (for full details of empirical studies see Parker and Heywood, 2000, and Heywood and Parker, 2001). The studies focused on forces, a traditionally difficult area of learning in science, and involved 30 teachers and 44 postgraduate trainees. The aim was to explore not only learners' perspectives of their own learning of the science in question but also the development of pedagogical knowledge that evolved as a result of this experience. A range of interactive strategies designed to foster engagement of learners with scientific ideas were used and these included:

- encouraging whole-class and group discussions of ideas in response to experiencing phenomena directly, raising questions and investigating emergent aspects;

- formulating personal hypotheses, testing and developing hypotheses and reformulating thinking as a result of critical scrutiny of evidence;
- orienting thinking within the context and becoming aware of their own reasoning, including areas of uncertainty about phenomena;
- having the opportunity to share intuitive responses and tacit knowledge;
- becoming aware of the similarities and differences between their own ideas and those of others, including scientific explanation;
- responding to and exploring hypothetical questions;
- modelling ideas and observing demonstrations;
- being introduced to analogies to explain behaviour and actively examining how useful these were in developing thinking;
- being introduced to cognitive challenge where evidence directly contradicts expectation;
- trying out ideas in different contexts.

Learning about forces requires learners to interpret scientific ideas that often do not fit with common-sense reasoning and the example illustrates the considerable expertise required of teachers in developing appropriate explanations. Teachers' learning in two contexts is explored: floating and sinking and bridges. Floating and sinking is a context commonly used at all levels in the foundation and primary education of children, often as a vehicle through which we provide primary children with experiences of forces acting on objects. In the following discussion no attempt is made to separate teachers and trainees unless stated explicitly and quotations are taken directly from learners' written or recorded reflections.

Initial conceptions

In order to engage thinking initially, teachers were asked to push an inflated balloon into a tank of water and discuss their observations and what they felt with respect to the forces they thought were acting. Responses often revealed a high level of general uncertainty:

> Why is it so difficult – is it the balloon or the water?

They tended to talk more of the water 'pushing back' and several viewed the experience as a 'battle of forces':

> The balloon resists the water as it battles the upthrust.

Some tried to explain their observations further:

> It's something to do with density and surface area.

Becoming aware of personal explanations is not always a straightforward process, as often there is a considerable degree of uncertainty in our thinking:

> Before I started I just knew what would float or sink but I'd forgotten why.

Becoming aware of personal explanations is an important element of learning. In reality it may take time for practical experience and discussion to articulate thinking and to become aware of areas of uncertainty. Preconceptions resemble theories-in-action and are expressed mainly upon use (Campanario, 2002). Indeed, on many occasions teachers are not fully aware of their own conceptions:

> I sort of know lots of things influence floating and sinking but I don't really know why, I'm not sure of anything.

> I have learned this in the past, about density, so I should know it.

The teachers identified the two opposing forces acting: 'push down' and upthrust. As a result of classroom experience, teachers were more likely to engage in discussion of forces than trainees. They were able to reason that when the balloon was resting on the water its weight still acted as a force in a downward direction, and that in a floating object such as this the downward force (weight) and the upthrust of the water must necessarily be balanced. However, there was an underlying unease when it came to *explaining* why some objects floated while others sank. In order to help clarify thinking, an activity was used to enable them to bring to bear their experience of floating and sinking. This is a common classroom activity involving predicting whether a selection of everyday objects would float or sink and then testing the predictions and reviewing the evidence. A brainstorm produced a list of factors that might influence whether an object would float or sink:

shape	air content	density	weight
material	surface area	solid/hollow	holes/gaps
size	surface tension	volume porosity	
mass	packing of molecules		

Some linked factors together like weight and surface area. It was interesting to note here that none of the factors identified related to forces. It is useful teacher knowledge to recognise that when thinking about floating and sinking a forces view is often alien to learners:

> I just didn't think about floating and sinking with a view to forces.

The activity enabled teachers to bring to bear life experience and personal reasoning. Particularly useful in promoting discussion was to focus on objects that behaved in a surprising way (e.g. the heavy block of wax that floated). It became apparent that there was a range of ideas and at this point teachers formulated personal hypotheses, for example:

> It's the air content that controls whether an object will float or sink.
> I think it's the weight but not alone, I think it's the surface area as well.

Not surprisingly weight formed a central tenet of thinking with 53% citing this as the determining factor. Air content (43%) and surface area (38%) also featured prominently. The next step in the quest for conceptual change was to test these hypotheses and to get the teachers to think about their own ideas in a critical way.

Conceptual change

If learning is an active process of personal construction whereby knowledge, understanding and experience of the world are integrated with new ideas and experiences, then it is the effectiveness of such integration and linking that ultimately determines the quality of learning. Research has focused on the search for a theoretical model of learning in an effort to identify factors influencing conceptual change in the hope of producing more effective teaching strategies. When ideas change, the nature of that change conforms to one of two patterns. *Assimilation*, in which learners' use existing concepts to deal with new phenomena, and *accommodation*, a process that requires their radical reorganisation or replacement. Learning may be a modification of existing concepts or a radical change. Limón and Mason's (2002) review of current thinking on how this process occurs explores several theoretical perspectives of conceptual change. Such perspectives view change as a process of repairing incorrect mental models. This requires organisation of complex knowledge systems through a process of synthesis, building a coherent explanatory framework that reconciles inconsistent explanatory models by integrating new material from science experiences with existing conceptual frameworks. A socio-cultural perspective views change requiring the use of appropriate cultural tools (intellectual tools such as concepts and physical tools such as artifacts) within relevant social activities. However, a pervasive, theoretical model of how conceptual change takes place remains elusive, reflecting the complexity and individual nature of learning.

Cognitive conflict

A key feature of conceptual change teaching is based on the premise that learners need to become dissatisfied with their existing ideas, thereby paving the way for the adoption of a more 'scientific' explanation. A commonly employed strategy in promoting such dissatisfaction is to introduce discrepant events that produce cognitive conflict. For example, weight played a central role in teachers' reasoning about why objects float or sink, yet we all *know* that heavy objects like ships do float. However, intuitive reasoning naturally focuses on weight as a determining factor: in everyday life heavy objects *do* tend to sink. Teachers associated a range of factors with the weight of the object (e.g. material the object is made from, air content, mass) and the size of the object (e.g. shape, volume, surface area) and in order to help clarify this they were deliberately presented with floating objects that were large and heavy (e.g. block of wood, large candle) and sinking objects that were light and small (e.g. paperclip, tiny ball of plasticene). As a result they began to make an association between weight *and* size in explaining floating and sinking. This was a critical step and a useful qualitative bridge to the scientific concept of density (mass/volume). It enabled them to reason about forces by exploring questions such as what would happen if the weight of the object was increased and the size kept constant and *vice versa* and to make sense of their tacit knowledge:

> It's just like a submarine isn't it, it makes itself heavier or lighter for its size, so it floats or sinks in the water.

However, simply introducing cognitive conflict into learning is no guarantee of conceptual change and research has shown that while it may produce a positive response in some learners, others fail to recognise the conflict or only partially resolve it using alternative conceptions (Tao and Gunstone, 2000). Responses may also be associated with the degree of commitment learners have to their existing ideas. For instance, this teacher remained committed to her notion that the air content of the object was the determining factor:

> Although you can't see it, there must be lots of air in the wood and the wax so that they can float.

Another teacher confirmed her misconception that the upward force resided in the water as an entity, its expression being determined by the amount of surface available for it to act on:

> Bigger objects have more surface for the force to push on.

Thus outcome of cognitive conflict depends on how the individual perceives and resolves that conflict. What is useful pedagogical knowledge for teachers, however, is how learners are likely to react to such conflict, what misconceptions might be reinforced by the experience and what useful constructs (e.g. the linking of weight and size) are likely to ensue.

At this point, the notion of a relationship between weight and size seemed to be potentially useful but as a new idea it needed to be tried out and explored further. Consequently, a focused investigation involving adding water to a screw-capped jar was used to focus thinking. Here the weight of the jar could be changed while keeping the size constant. It could be made heavier or lighter *for its size*, thereby embedding the relationship through direct investigation. It was interesting to note that at this point teachers often began to reason spontaneously about the forces acting (Figure 4.1).

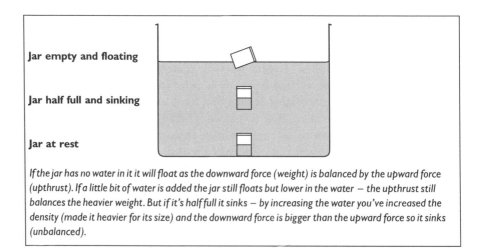

> If the jar has no water in it it will float as the downward force (weight) is balanced by the upward force (upthrust). If a little bit of water is added the jar still floats but lower in the water – the upthrust still balances the heavier weight. But if it's half full it sinks – by increasing the water you've increased the density (made it heavier for its size) and the downward force is bigger than the upward force so it sinks (unbalanced).

Figure 4.1. Adding water to a screw-capped jar

Context-dependent/independent change

A characteristic of the learning process is that learning that takes place in one context is often not transferred successfully by learners to another context (Tao and Gunstone, 2000). For example, a child might identify shadow formation as a result of blocking the light from a torch but fail to recognise the same process with regard to their own shadow in the playground. This became apparent in the forces study and it was possible to identify key points at which teachers experienced difficulty in transferring concepts across contexts (Heywood and Parker, 2001). Learners' perceptions of their own learning revealed key ideas retained from floating and sinking and how they applied them in other forces contexts such as static structures (e.g. bridges) and motion, both vertical and horizontal. Key ideas identified were:

- **weight is a downward force;**
- **gravity is a downward force;**
- **water exerts an upthrust/upward force;**
- **forces are unbalanced in sinking objects;**
- **forces act in pairs and in opposite directions;**
- **forces are in balance in floating objects;**
- **the relationship of weight to size determines floating.**

When asked to apply their reasoning to a simple arched bridge model that was progressively loaded until it eventually collapsed, most recognised weight as a downward acting force (Figure 4.2).

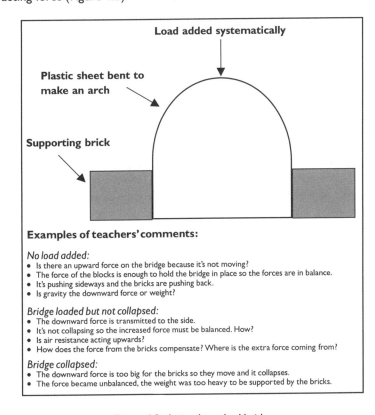

Load added systematically

Plastic sheet bent to make an arch

Supporting brick

Examples of teachers' comments:

No load added:
- Is there an upward force on the bridge because it's not moving?
- The force of the blocks is enough to hold the bridge in place so the forces are in balance.
- It's pushing sideways and the bricks are pushing back.
- Is gravity the downward force or weight?

Bridge loaded but not collapsed:
- The downward force is transmitted to the side.
- It's not collapsing so the increased force must be balanced. How?
- Is air resistance acting upwards?
- How does the force from the bricks compensate? Where is the extra force coming from?

Bridge collapsed:
- The downward force is too big for the bricks so they move and it collapses.
- The force became unbalanced, the weight was too heavy to be supported by the bricks.

Figure 4.2. A simple arched bridge

They talked about the downward force increasing as the load increased. As the bridge did not collapse they reasoned that there must be an equal and opposite counteracting force but many wrestled with the notion, struggling to explain where this force would come from. They also struggled to explain how the bridge continued to support an increasing load without collapse:

> How does the bridge know how much force to push back with?

Again the misconception of force as an entity belonging to or residing in an object emerges. The context of the static bridge, although appearing to be a similar situation in terms of balanced and unbalanced forces to floating and sinking (supporting the load/floating and collapsing/sinking), was fundamentally different in that:

- **there was no obvious force counteracting the downward force of weight;**
- **there was no direct tactile experience;**
- **it required learners to envisage forces acting sideways in the structure – this contradicted their notion of forces acting in opposite directions.**

The more complicated the structure (e.g. suspension bridge) the more the learners struggled to apply their reasoning. However, important pedagogical knowledge for teachers lay in being able to recognise that the new context (bridges) placed further demand on learning and that what is needed is a refocusing of questioning and experiences that enable learners to explore these difficulties directly. For instance, consideration of the nature of materials and how they behave when loaded, leading ultimately to a consideration of chemical bonding and forces acting between molecules, might constitute a logical next step. Clearly, there is a danger in assuming that concepts that appear to have been internalised in one context can be applied directly and without problem in different contexts.

Developing coherent causal explanations

For conceptual change to occur learners must adopt a different explanation of a phenomenon. The new explanation must make sense, be more plausible and applicable to a variety of contexts. As existing conceptions arise from a wealth of life experience there needs to be good reason to change or modify them. Changes must entail cognitive advantage such as a deeper understanding of a subject as opposed to just having knowledge of it. For instance, the linking of weight and size in a relationship proved to be very fruitful for many learners and was clear evidence of them *trying out* this changed explanation:

- **salt water would give a heavier weight to move so the jar would float higher;**
- **if we put helium in instead of air it would be lighter and float higher;**
- **it's a bit like trying to see how good it is – if it fits in lots of ways.**

Meaningful explanation lies at the heart of the scientific endeavour as well as learning and, therefore, science education. Explanations that show a clear cause and effect are highly valued by learners because they contain considerable explanatory power (Gilbert et al., 1988a) and are, therefore, more likely to lead towards context-independent conceptual change.

Synthesising subject and pedagogy

Teachers' reflections revealed a host of pedagogical implications for practice:

- the abstract nature of forces and pushes and pulls and the need to make sense of them through physical experience;
- personal constructs are not always clear and there are often areas of uncertainty in thinking (thinking about personal ideas takes time, orientation and confidence);
- weight is central in people's reasoning despite contradictory knowledge from real situations and teaching needs to address this;
- people rarely use a forces explanation of floating and sinking in explaining events;
- learning needs to move beyond simple prediction and testing into meaningful explanation;
- meaningful explanation enables learners to make sense of life experience;
- explanation needs to be applicable to a range of contexts;
- explanation requires the linking together of two factors: weight and size;
- the need to relate the qualitative explanation (weight for size) to personal knowledge of density (a quantitative explanation);
- the need to structure learning so that it enables learners to make sense of observations in a developmental way;
- the opportunity afforded by experiences to reinforce misconceptions such as air makes things float;
- how learning is often difficult to transfer to different situations and learners will need support in doing this.

Of course not all teachers and trainees identified all of the points above and some made even more progress producing insightful comments including:

> I now feel there is a lot more to understanding floating and sinking than I first imagined ... it's the building of ideas and putting them together ... holding two ideas together is much harder than holding them separately.

These pedagogical insights are specific to developing an understanding of forces acting in floating and sinking but other features of the learning process are more general and include aspects of the learning process:

- the value of talk and social interaction in science learning;
- the usefulness of focusing on the similarities and differences between the ranges of explanation (including currently accepted scientific thinking);
- the effectiveness of the tension created between competing concepts in promoting discussion, fuelling the need to resolve uncertainties and leading towards conceptual convergence;
- the formulation of personal hypotheses entails careful scrutiny of personal ideas and the opportunity to test thinking through practical exploration provides evidence to reformulate thinking;
- appreciation of the cognitive learning demand inherent in subject matter.

Of course many of these general features of the learning process identified by the teachers have long been recognised as significant in developing understanding in science education. For example, the SPACE project (1990–1998) identified a range of important pedagogical implications for children's learning, including the importance of engaging with children's ideas through testing personal ideas, focusing on developing the meaning of language and the importance of promoting the generalisation of concepts. As with the teachers in the study, investigation emerged as an important part of learning:

> The investigation let us test to see which of our ideas worked, I could see why mine didn't.

This is an altogether more subtle view of the role of scientific investigations that enables teachers to understand more thoroughly the implications of scientific enquiry. For a teacher who holds a view of science as a process of factual transmission, recognising the value of investigation in learning is crucial.

Curricular expertise:

a summary of key points

— *The drive towards achieving the standards in qualifying to teach and raising standards of science teaching in school implies not only a sufficient level of teacher science subject knowledge but also a professional repertoire appropriate to supporting children's learning effectively in the classroom. These two aspects are necessarily linked and effective practice is a synthesis of both.*

— *An increased part of pre-service training now takes place in school where teacher mentors working in partnership with ITT tutors have greater responsibility for the professional development and assessment of trainees. This includes a responsibility for challenging and developing trainees' understanding of the science concepts they are teaching. Thus, the dramatic changes towards primary science education witnessed during the past 15 years have placed considerable demand on teachers' science curricular expertise.*

— *Primary teachers have made tremendous progress from a profession generally lacking in confidence in terms of science education at the advent of the National Curriculum to an effective teaching force achieving high levels of attainment in statutory tests. This has been achieved through a combination of in-service training, staff development within schools and the accumulation of experience gained in working with children in classrooms. Some areas of science still remain somewhat problematic, however. In particular, the scientific enquiry and the physical sciences present difficulty for some teachers in the later stages of Key Stage 2. The latter is probably to do with the abstract and counter-intuitive nature of scientific ideas inherent in scientific explanations in this area, an aspect of science education that needs to be recognised more widely in future if effective learning is to take place.*

How then might teachers develop their curricular expertise in science? There is a range of avenues open to individuals seeking to do so:

- *Developing science subject knowledge. There are currently several publications aimed at helping primary teachers to audit and test their science subject knowledge, including the nature of science (e.g. Peacock, 1998; Sharp and Byrne, 2003). Once weaknesses have been identified there are a variety of background knowledge books aimed at teachers and trainees (e.g. Sharp et al., 2002; Hollins and Whitby, 2001) and an increasing number of websites aimed at primary teachers;*
- *Developing science pedagogical knowledge. There is a range of materials to help teachers develop their practice which they contain useful advice on children's learning in science and strategies for eliciting their ideas and supporting learning (e.g. Harlen, 2000; Johnsey et al., 2002; Keogh et al., 2002). As well as these there is a range of official documents produced by the Teacher Training Agency and other sources.*
- *Selecting appropriate in-service training. Schools need to consider the type of training that will best support teachers in developing curricular expertise in science. Research indicates that training that engages teachers directly in the conceptual change process is more likely to result in a deeper understanding of scientific explanations. The example of teachers learning about forces illustrated shows that through critical reflection on their own learning process, teachers generate valuable pedagogical insight into the learning of science concepts. Such a metacognitive approach, however, if in the form of a single event, is unlikely to result in sustained changes in thinking or practice. Training needs to be considered as a cycle of continuing professional development in which theory integrates and informs practice.*

The case presented here suggests that effective teaching can be promoted by science education that explores the subtleties of learning within specific scientific domains in which both pedagogy and subject are synthesised. As we continue in the new millennium science teacher education is poised to develop further. For example, a new £51m DfES and Wellcome Trust initiative to set up Science Learning Centres throughout the country is a very welcome step forward. These new centres are designed to inspire teachers and to build upon their professional skills in an attempt to invigorate science in the classroom. The initiative offers opportunity for a synthesis of research and teaching in which teachers can reflect on their own learning of science in order to identify key issues in subject and pedagogical knowledge, consequently broadening and deepening the knowledge bases that underpin curricular expertise within the profession.

5 THE SCIENCE CURRICULUM

JOHN SHARP AND ROB BOWKER

Introduction

The introduction of a National Curriculum of subjects to all maintained schools throughout England and Wales in 1989 brought compulsory science education into the primary sector for the first time. As a direct result of its elevated profile, and an immense amount of hard work and effort by those involved at the 'chalk-face' in particular, science education provision benefited enormously. Since then, however, successive 'overhauls' of the primary science curriculum have brought about many changes, some not necessarily for the better or resulting in improvement. In this chapter, we present a critical account of the development and evolution of science in the primary school and, taking astronomy as an example, draw attention to the need for care at times when classroom practices and expectations are driven by 'national science curricula' which remain to be fully informed. For those readers new to the profession, entering it for perhaps the first time or still undergoing training and for whom the National Curriculum is perhaps regarded as a 'way of life', the account presented here might present something of a surprise.

Historical background

According to most sources, the teaching of science in primary schools in England and Wales can be traced back to at least the 1870s when it was almost entirely restricted to the study of nature. Curiously, and despite some expansion reflected in two major curriculum projects, *Nuffield Junior Science* (1964–1966) and *Science 5–13* (1967–1974), nature studies continued to dominate most primary science until well into the 1970s. At that time, and against a widespread 'progressivist orientation' towards teaching and learning as a whole (child-centred, discovery-led and process-driven), the influential and widely quoted *National Primary Survey* of schools considered science education provision to be far from satisfactory (DES, 1978):

- **the range of science experienced by children was often too narrow and the overall standard of work generally poor;**
- **science coverage was often superficial with science teaching less well matched to the capabilities of children than in other curriculum areas;**
- **science was either neglected as part of the primary curriculum or often integrated within other subjects and 'lost' in the teaching of broad topics;**
- **financial and logistical support for science was often insufficient;**
- **a detailed knowledge and understanding of science among primary teachers themselves was often limited.**

Only later with the publication of *Science in Primary Schools* (DES, 1983), the seminal *Science 5–16: A Statement of Policy* (DES/WO, 1985) and *The Curriculum from 5 to 16* (DES, 1989) were the goals and expectations of science in primary schools clearly expressed and articulated, perhaps for the first time in almost a century of science teaching. Science, it was said, should 'foster a range of desirable personal qualities including curiosity and healthy scepticism, respect for the environment, the critical evaluation of evidence, an appreciation of a significant part of our cultural heritage, and an insight into man's (sic) place in the world'. The importance of breadth, balance and relevance was emphasised.

Pause for thought

The place of science in the school curriculum

Strange though it may seem, there is no a priori reason for science to appear in the curriculum of any primary school, nationally formulated or not. The intrinsic nature of science, including how it satisfies human curiosity with reliable knowledge, is, however, particularly compelling. While many review the justification of school science on sound economic, utilitarian, democratic, social, cultural and other arguments, Chapman (1994) has suggested that such arguments are weak and that the importance of a science education at school is often overstated. Considering these different arguments, reflect on your own views of primary science and the purpose it serves. What is a science education for? Whose views are important and why? What should a science curriculum contain and how should it be presented? Who should deliver the curriculum and how should they be selected and prepared? What is meant by standards in science education and how should these be measured?

Growing discontent

Laudable though it might be, it would be naive in the extreme to believe that the idea of a National Curriculum for primary science arose solely from the concerns over its status presented earlier. Instead, the idea of a National Curriculum for primary science, arose elsewhere. According to Moon (1994), for example, by the end of the 1970s, the government of the day became particularly disillusioned with the educational establishment as a whole, and the 'progressive' nature of primary education, from the planning, teaching and assessment of individual lessons to the organisation and management of classrooms, came increasingly under attack. The increased central and political interest in education eventually culminated in the Education Reform Act of 1988 within which provision for a National Curriculum of subjects was established. Such was the importance of science it was included alongside English and mathematics in what became referred to simply as 'the core'.

Science and the National Curriculum

To date, there have been four 'final' versions of primary science within the National Science Curriculum as a whole, and the 'struggle' to formulate it over the years since its introduction has been well documented. An overview of the different versions is provided in Table 5.1.

Science in the National Curriculum (DES/WO 1989)	Science in the National Curriculum (DES/WO 1991)	Science in the National Curriculum (DfE/WO 1995)	Science: the National Curriculum for England (DfEE/QCA 1999)
Attainment Targets	*Attainment Targets and strands*	*Programmes of Study with strands*	*Programmes of Study with strands*
AT1: Exploration of science AT2: The variety of life AT3: Processes of life AT4: Genetics and evolution AT5: Human influences on the Earth AT6: Types and uses of materials AT7: Making new materials AT8: Explaining how materials behave AT9: Earth and atmosphere AT10: Forces AT11: Electricity and magnetism AT12: Scientific aspects of IT AT13: Energy AT14: Sound and music AT15: Using light and EM radiation AT16: The Earth in space AT17: The nature of science	AT1: Scientific investigation (i) question, predict, hypothesise (ii) observe, measure and manipulate variables iii) interpret results and evaluate evidence AT2: Life and living processes (i) life processes and the organisation of living things (ii) variation and mechanisms of inheritance and evolution (iii) populations and human influences within ecosystems (iv) energy flows and cycles of matter within ecosystems AT3: Materials and their properties (i) the properties, classification and structure of materials (ii) explanations of the properties of materials (iii) chemical changes (iv) the Earth and its atmosphere AT4: Physical processes (i) electricity and magnetism (ii) energy resources and transfer (iii) forces and their effects (iv) light and sound (v) the Earth's place in the universe	Sc1: Experimental and investigative science 1. planning experimental work 2. obtaining evidence 3. considering evidence Sc2: Life processes and living things 1. life processes 2. humans as organisms 3. green plants as organisms 4. variation and classification 5. living things in their environment Sc3: Materials and their properties 1. grouping and classifying materials 2. changing materials 3. separating mixtures of materials Sc4: Physical processes 1. electricity 2. forces and motion 3. light and sound 4. the Earth and beyond	Sc1: Scientific enquiry ideas and evidence in science; investigative skills Sc2: Life processes and living things life processes; humans and other animals; green plants; variation and classification Sc3: Materials and their properties grouping and classifying materials; changing materials; separating mixtures of materials Sc4: Physical processes electricity; forces and motion; light and sound; the Earth and beyond
ATs 7, 8 and 14 KS2 only		Sc3.3 and Sc4.4 KS2 only	Sc3 separating mixtures of materials and Sc4 the Earth and beyond KS2 only
Programmes of Study placed after Attainment Targets and Statements of Attainment	*Programmes of Study placed alongside Attainment Targets and Statements of Attainment*	*Attainment Targets and level descriptions placed after Programmes of Study*	*Attainment Targets and level descriptions placed after Programmes of Study*

Table 5.1. Overview of 'final' versions of the National Curriculum for primary science

The Science Working Group

The National Science Curriculum began to take form with a Science Working Group of respected science educators and other professionals in 1987 in anticipation of the Education Reform Act of 1988 and its contents. The Science Working Group was briefed to recommend Programmes of Study (PoS), which would set out the science that children should be taught, Attainment Targets (ATs), which would set out the science that children should know and be able to do, and a framework of Levels and Statements of Attainment (LoA and SoA) for the purposes of assessment and reporting. Like the other core subjects, the primary science component was considered in terms of two periods of schooling: Key Stage 1 (5- to 7-year-olds in Years 1 and 2) and Key Stage 2 (7- to 11-year-olds in Years 3 to 6). The Science Working Group was conscious of 'breaking new ground' and acknowledged the lack of trialling and inadequate research available to it in certain areas as problematic.

Version 1

Following consultation, the *first version* of the National Science Curriculum was published (DES/WO, 1989). This was front-loaded with 17 different Attainment Targets, each with its own Levels and Statements of Attainment set out in the form of a linear assessment scale, and supporting Programmes of Study. The 17 Attainment Targets were grouped into two Profile Components (PCs). At both Key Stages 1 and 2, AT1: Exploration of science (Profile Component 1) contained explicit reference to children planning, hypothesising, predicting, designing and carrying out their own investigations, identifying and quantifying variables and constructing fair tests. ATs 2 to 16 (Profile Component 2) reflected the content of science.

Version 2

Soon after the appearance of the first version, however, an urgent review of the structure of the National Science Curriculum was undertaken. The 17 Attainment Targets were thought to provide an obstacle to manageable and sound testing and intelligible reporting to parents and, for secondary school requirements, the consistency of GCSE examination standards was considered at risk unless the number of Attainment Targets was reduced. Proposed revisions went to consultation. In the *second version* (DES/WO, 1991), the 17 Attainment Targets were reduced to four with associated strands reflecting a more traditionally familiar science curriculum dominated by biology, chemistry and physics. AT1: Scientific investigation replaced AT1: Exploration of science but retained its original focus. Programmes of Study were placed alongside the Attainment Targets rather than after them. Within the two primary Key Stages, the original 158 individual Statements of Attainment were 'simplified' and reduced to 58 with some 'shuffling' of position at particular levels. The two Profile Components were considered unnecessary and removed.

Version 3

Between the second and third versions, the entire National Curriculum of subjects and its assessment were reviewed to identify scope for even further 'slimming', to reconsider the linear assessment scale operating throughout all four Key Stages (primary and secondary), to simplify testing arrangements, to improve the overall burden of administration, to continue to remove unhelpful areas of overlap between Key Stages and across subjects, and to rectify any known areas of weakness (Dearing, 1993). In the *third version* (DfE/WO, 1995), Programmes of Study were placed before the Attainment Targets and identified by their 'Sc' designation. Level descriptions replaced Statements of Attainment but were less specific. The linear assessment scale was retained but reduced in scope. Sc1: Experimental and investigative science replaced AT1: Scientific investigation. While this remained isolated, some technical requirements were relaxed.

Version 4

Under a brief of 'minimal change', and following a five-year moratorium on curriculum development, a *fourth version* of the National Science Curriculum soon made its appearance (DfEE/QCA, 1999). The most notable change involved Sc1: Experimental and investigative science becoming Sc1: Scientific enquiry. The values, aims and purposes of the National Curriculum as a whole were clarified and the place and nature of science within it strengthened. Around this time, an exemplary, though not statutory, *Scheme of Work for Science at Key Stages 1 and 2* also made its appearance (QCA/DfEE, 1998, with amendments, 2000).

Pause for thought

Curriculum models

According to Kelly (1999), a curriculum may be designed around a delivered syllabus, a series of short-term teaching objectives and learning outcomes, or long-term broad educational goals. The National Curriculum for primary science, within the context of the National Curriculum as a whole, reflects a complex interaction of competing model types. As Kelly and others have pointed out, while it is certainly useful and advantageous to base a curriculum around a syllabus of sorts, together with associated teaching objectives and learning outcomes which are easy to assess, as is most apparent in the design of the National Curriculum for primary science, this can, however, result in a completely stifled, static and mechanistic view of teaching and an overly simplistic notion of education and standards. To what extent do you think this position is justified?

Curriculum concerns

Following its introduction, teachers eventually adjusted to the new requirements and the demands placed upon them to translate and transform policy into practice. It quickly became clear, however, that interpretations of requirements and implementation strategies varied widely from school to school and class to class (Carré and Carter, 1990, 1993). According to many sources (e.g. Oakley, 1993; Jenkins, 1995; Black, 1995; Ritchie, 1996):

- the initial overemphasis placed on Attainment Targets, driven by Levels and Statements of Attainment and the assessment framework, tended to 'spoil' the science by overly narrowing its focus;

- the initial overemphasis on content conflicted with the integrated nature of topic work common to primary practice at that time;
- many teachers were initially 'disorientated' by the more advanced requirements of ATI which went ahead of current practice and expertise and practical work began to focus on 'consumer-type' and 'variable-type' fair-tests which either involved little use of scientific principles at all or presented a rather narrow and unrepresentative view of how scientists actually work;
- teachers had little experience of selecting investigative tasks that were well matched to children's abilities and usefully linked to concept and skills development;
- provision for the nature of science, with the need to improve scientific literacy for public understanding, remained inadequate;
- reform focused more on aspects of curriculum manageability and assessment administration rather than on the nature and essence of science provision itself and the actual day-to-day needs of primary teachers and the children they teach.

As noted by Harlen (1992a), while the purposes, goals and expectations of a curriculum may well be stated for political as well as educational reasons, there is often a considerable difference between national policies and what happens in schools where ideals might never be approached in practice.

Out of this world

Some of the changes and challenges encountered at their most extreme are perhaps best exemplified by considering the 'fate' of astronomy. Astronomy 'succeeded' in making it into the National Science Curriculum after it first appeared as a component of Earth, atmosphere and space, one of five original themes proposed by the Science Working Group in 1987. Despite no real history and tradition of astronomy teaching in the primary sector, its inclusion nevertheless acknowledged a long overdue attempt to capitalise on children's undoubted interest and curiosity in this field and to enrich their experiences of science as a whole.

The rise and fall

In the *first version* of the National Science Curriculum (DES/WO, 1989), astronomy was identified as ATI6: The Earth in space (see Table 5.2). In its original form, teachers were obliged to ensure that children across the primary age phase explored a variety of astronomical features and phenomena. At Key Stage 1 (5 to 7 years), infants were expected to investigate plants, animals and the weather within their own locality and relate any changes observed to the passage of time. They were also expected to know about the Earth, the Sun and the Moon as separate, spherical objects. At Key Stage 2 (7 to 11 years), juniors were expected to investigate the night sky through direct observation and by using secondary sources, and to use a simple model of the solar system and Earth–Sun–Moon system to attempt explanations of the day and night cycle, seasonal change and the phases of the Moon. Though easily questionable and open to challenge in terms of actual content and the relative importance ascribed to individual age-linked statements within it, something of a promising start had been made. Within only two years, astronomy looked very different. ATI6: The

DES/WO (1989) AT16: The Earth in space	DES/WO (1991) AT4: Physical processes (v) the Earth's place in the universe	DfE/WO (1995) Sc4: Physical processes	DfEE/QCA (1999) Sc4: Physical processes
KS1 Statements of Attainment Children should: Level 1 • be able to describe through talking, or other appropriate means, the seasonal changes that occur in the weather and in living things; • know the danger of looking directly at the Sun; • be able to describe, in relation to their home or school, the apparent daily motion of the Sun across the sky. Level 2 • be able to explain why night occurs; • know that day length changes throughout the year; • know that we live on a large, spherical, self-contained planet, called Earth; • know that the Earth, Moon and Sun are separate bodies. Level 3 • know that the inclination of the Sun in the sky changes during the year; • be able to measure time with a sundial. *KS1 Programme of Study (placed after AT and SoA)* Children should observe closely their local natural environment to detect seasonal changes, including day length, weather and changes in plants and animals, and relate these to the passage of time. They should observe, over a period of time, the length of the day, the position of the Sun, and where possible the Moon, in the sky. They should investigate the use of a sundial as a means of observing the passage of time.	*KS1 Statements of Attainment* Children should: Level 1 • be able to describe the apparent movement of the Sun across the sky. Level 2 • know that the Earth, Sun and Moon are separate spherical bodies. Level 3 • know that the appearance of the Moon and the altitude of the Sun change in a regular and predictable manner. *KS1 Programme of Study (placed alongside AT and SoA)* Children should observe closely the local natural environment to detect seasonal changes, including length of daylight, weather and changes in plants and animals and relate these to the passage of time. They should observe, over a period of time, the length of daylight, the position of the Sun, and when possible the position of the Moon in the sky and its changing appearance.	Withdrawn	Withdrawn

Table 5.2 Astronomy education provision throughout 'final' versions of the National Curriculum for primary science

DES/WO (1989) AT16: The Earth in space	DES/WO (1991) AT4: Physical processes (v) the Earth's place in the universe	DfE/WO (1995) Sc4: Physical processes 4. the Earth and beyond	DfEE/QCA (1999) Sc4: Physical processes the Earth and beyond
KS2 Statements of Attainment Children should: Levels 2 and 3 are as KS1 Level 4 • know that the phases of the Moon change in a regular and predictable manner; • know that the solar system is made up of the Sun and planets, and have an idea of its scale; • understand that the Sun is a star. Level 5 • be able to relate a simple model of the solar system to day and night and year length, changes of day length, seasonal changes and changes in the inclination of the Sun.	KS2 Statements of Attainment Children should: Levels 2 and 3 are as KS1 Level 4 • be able to explain day and night, day length and year length in terms of the movements of the Earth around the Sun. Level 5 • be able to describe the motion of the planets in the solar system. KS2 Programme of Study (placed after AT and SoA) Children should be given opportunities to investigate changes in the night sky, in particular the position of the Moon, through direct observation and by using secondary sources. Children should use a simple model of the solar system to attempt explanations of day and night, year length and changes in the aspect of the Moon and elevation of the Sun. They should be introduced to the principle of the sundial as a means of noting the passage of time. They should learn about the position and motion of the Earth, Moon and Sun relative to each other.	KS2 Programme of Study Children should be taught: (a) that the Sun, Earth and Moon are approximately spherical; (b) that the position of the Sun appears to change during the day, and how shadows change as this happens; (c) that the Earth spins around its own axis, and how day and night are related to this spin; (d) that the Earth orbits the Sun once a year, and that the Moon takes approximately 28 days to orbit the Earth. AT4: level descriptions (placed after PoS) Level 1 • children recognise that light comes from a variety of sources and name some. Level 2 • children know about a range of physical phenomena and recognise and describe similarities and differences associated with them. Level 3 • children use physical ideas to explain simple phenomena; • children make simple generalisations about physical phenomena. Level 4 • children describe, explain and make generalisations about physical phenomena. Level 5 • children apply and use some abstract ideas in descriptions of physical phenomena; • children use models to explain effects observed with physical phenomena.	KS2 Programme of Study Children should be taught: (a) that the Sun, Earth and Moon are approximately spherical; (b) how the position of the Sun appears to change during the day, and how shadows change as this happens; (c) how day and night are related to the spin of the Earth on its own axis; (d) that the Earth orbits the Sun once each year, and that the Moon takes approximately 28 days to orbit the Earth. AT4: level descriptions (placed after PoS) Level 1 • children recognise that light comes from a variety of sources and name some. Level 2 • children know about a range of physical phenomena and recognise and describe similarities and differences associated with them. Level 3 • children use physical ideas to explain simple phenomena; • children make simple generalisations about physical phenomena. Level 4 • children describe, explain and make generalisations about physical phenomena. Level 5 • children apply and use some abstract ideas in descriptions of physical phenomena; • children use models to explain effects observed with physical phenomena.

KS2 Programme of Study (placed alongside AT and SoA)

Children should track the path of the Sun using safe procedures such as a shadow stick or sundial. They should study, using direct observations where possible, the night sky including the position and appearance of bright planets and the Moon. They should learn about the motions of the Earth, Moon and Sun in order to explain day and night, day length, year length, phases of the Moon, eclipses and the seasons. They should be introduced to the order and general movements of the planets around the Sun.

Table 5.2 (cont.)

Earth in space became strand (v) the Earth's place in the universe within AT4: Physical processes (DES/WO, 1991). Requirements to explain why night occurs at Level 2 moved to a broader statement about day and night at Level 4 and initial reference to the solar system at Level 4 moved to Level 5. By the appearance of the *third version* (DfE/WO, 1995), more alarming developments had taken place. All Key Stage 1 astronomy requirements had been moved to Key Stage 2 and these were more tightly focused on the Earth–Sun–Moon System. All reference to the solar system and wider universe was delayed to Key Stage 3. Astronomy in the *fourth version* (DfEE/QCA, 1999) remained largely unchanged. Despite consultation, few reasons were ever provided to adequately account for the changes observed though some subject overlap and territorialism between science and geography and a general lack of science-specific curricular expertise throughout the primary profession undoubtedly contributed (Russell *et al.*, 1995). Quite bizarrely, and in the formulation of the *third version*, it was actually indicated that astronomy should be removed from Key Stage 1 to offset the increase in content as a result of reinstating electricity which had been overlooked earlier! More worryingly, perhaps, the revisions appeared to either contradict or ignore findings presented in the first commissioned evaluation of the National Science Curriculum and its implementation (Russell *et al.*, 1994) as well as those findings concerning how children learn astronomy produced independently.

Evidence-based research

Interestingly, and given the speed and extent of educational reform and curriculum development in England and Wales, the first published study to begin to consider children's ideas in astronomy appeared in the same year as the National Science Curriculum itself (Baxter, 1989). While some valuable research from the United States, Israel and Nepal was also available (e.g. Klein, 1982; Jones *et al.*, 1987; Nussbaum, 1985), this was clearly insufficient for the national task at hand. Despite now having a better indication of the state of development of children's ideas in astronomy and the implications for teaching and learning across the entire primary age phase (e.g. Vosniadou, 1991; Vosniadou and Brewer, 1992, 1994; Osborne *et al.*, 1994; Sharp, 1995, 1996; Kikas, 1998; Sneider and Ohady, 1998; Diakidoy and Kendeou, 2001), much work still remains to be done. What has emerged so far is a clear view that children are not only capable of learning astronomy, they are capable of learning it very well indeed despite the non-spontaneous and counter-intuitive nature of most of its traditional subject matter (the Earth, Sun and Moon, the Earth–Sun–Moon System, the solar system and wider universe).

By way of example, snapshot findings from a detailed study of knowledge acquisition and concept learning in astronomy among thirty-one 9- to 11-year-olds attending a primary school in the south-west of England are presented. Here, all of the children involved were taught astronomy by their own class teacher, an experienced primary practitioner with a positive attitude and constructivist orientation towards science. Throughout the 10 two-hour astronomy lessons negotiated, the children were involved in sharing each other's ideas, the ideas of people who lived in the past and the ideas of the scientific community today, obtaining, considering and evaluating primary and other sources of information, including that from extended day- and night-time observations of the sky (the latter as homework), and using concrete scientific models. The children, together with some of their parents, also participated in an evening trip to a local observatory. All of the children had experienced National Curriculum astronomy earlier in Key Stage I. From a mixed starting point in terms of the range and type of ideas elicited at interview before teaching, significantly greater levels of scientific conceptualisation were recorded afterwards. Progression was most evident in the children's use of scientific vocabulary, in their drawings, in their ability to model the Earth–Sun–Moon System using props, particularly to illustrate the day and night cycle, and in their thinking and reasoning skills. The retention of scientific ideas after a brief delay of three months was also notable (see Table 5.3). Despite the advances made, the presentation of scientific models of seasonal change and the phases of the Moon remained the exception throughout. Findings such as these tell us much about the teaching and learning of astronomy and its place in the curriculum:

	Immediately before teaching	Immediately after teaching	Three months after teaching
Earth shape	29 (93.5)	31 (100.0)	31 (100.0)
Sun shape	25 (80.6)	28 (90.3)	28 (90.3)
Moon shape	20 (64.5)	26 (83.9)	27 (87.1)
Relative size	14 (45.2)	25 (80.6)	26 (83.9)
Day and night	11 (35.5)	24 (77.4)	23 (74.2)
Seasonal change	0 (0.0)	15 (48.4)	9 (29.0)
Moon's phases	0 (0.0)	15 (48.4)	7 (22.6)
Solar system (map)	1 (3.2)	22 (71.0)	19 (61.3)

Table 5.3. Frequencies and percentages of correct scientific
ideas presented at interview (n=31)

- while acknowledging some of the conceptual and procedural demands imposed upon individuals as astronomical information increases in complexity and conflicts with everyday experience, astronomy can nevertheless be made readily accessible to children provided it is presented to them in a developmentally appropriate way and at a developmentally appropriate time;
- progression towards attaining scientific conceptualisation in most content areas can be 'facilitated' or 'accelerated' by encountering those areas as infants in Key Stage I and revisiting them again later;
- conventional wisdom which advocates teaching astronomy sequentially by moving away from the Earth to the Earth-Sun-Moon system to the solar system and wider universe is not consistent with the sequence of learning it;
- many children, boys and girls, often display a more positive attitude towards astronomy than many other areas of science experienced by them.

Individual responses were also particularly revealing. Ian, for example, was 10 years and 11 months old at the time of being interviewed after having been taught (I = Ian; R = Researcher). As far as could be ascertained, Ian was an 'average' child in every respect. His comments about the true shape of the Earth being 'like a sphere' but bulging out at the equator, how we might test the notion of a spherical Sun and the effects of the Moon's gravity would certainly put most adults to shame! In this example, Ian's freehand drawings of what causes day and night, the seasons to change and the phases of the Moon from memory were also advanced (recall, detail, spatial representation Figure 5.1). Despite the advanced nature of Ian's responses, many errors and ideas derived from alternative interpretational frameworks remained (use your own knowledge and understanding of astronomy to spot them).

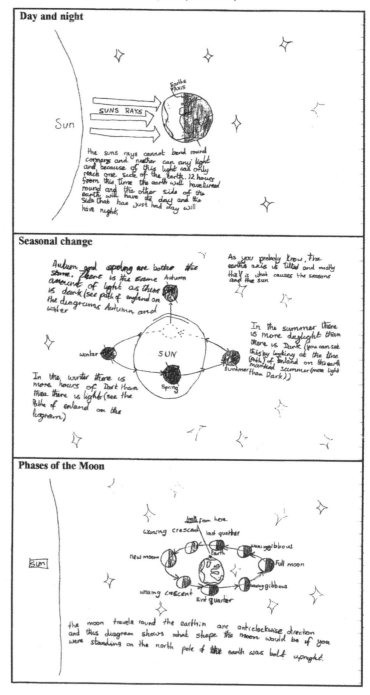

Figure 5.1. Ian's freehand drawings of Earth–Sun–Moon System phenomena

The Earth

R: What shape is the Earth?

I: It's like a sphere. [Explored.] *Because the equator comes out more than the rest of the Earth ... it bulges out.*

R: Is there a shape here that's most like the Earth [selection provided]?

I: *That one.* [Picks a sphere.]

R: How do people know it's that shape?

I: *Because they've been up in space rockets and they've sent up satellites.*

R: Can you draw a picture of what you think the Earth would look like from space? [Draws a circle with identifiable land masses.]

R: What colour would it be?

I: *Green* [land], *blue* [water], *white for clouds, yellow for deserts, white at the poles.*

R: Have you ever heard of anybody falling off the Earth?

I: *No.* [Laughs.] *Yes maybe in the Bermuda Triangle.* [Laughs.]

R: Could anybody ever fall off the Earth?

I: *Not unless they could jump into a space rocket ... because there's lots of gravity and it pulls you down to the Earth like this* [picks up a sphere and lets it go].

R: What is the Earth?

I: *It's a planet. It's like a rock.*

The Sun

R: What is the Sun?

I: *It's a big ball of burning gas.*

R: What shape is the Sun?

I: *A sphere.*

R: Is there a shape here that's most like the Sun [selection provided]?

I: *This one.* [Picks a sphere.]

R: How do people know it's that shape?

I: *Because as we go round ... unless the Sun turns like this as we go round it it's the same shape* [picks up a disk for the Sun and a sphere for the Earth to demonstrate how a disk must rotate in order to maintain apparent shape]. *They could launch a rocket to see if was like this* [disk] *or if it was this shape* [compares a sphere with shapes having circular outlines].

R: Can you draw a picture of what you think the Sun would look like from space? [Draws a circle with *'flares'* and dark spots referred to as *'cooler areas of gas'.*]

R: What colour would it be?

I: *Orange, yellow and red.*

R: Does anything live on the Sun?

I: *No ... it's far too hot.* [Explored.] *It's about six thousand degrees on the outside and about fifteen million in the inside.* [Explored.] *It's gas ... mm ... burning gas ... mm ... helium gas it might be. It's fuelling the Sun. It started by ... it ... the Sun was really big and starting pulling things in really fast. It just started like a nuclear bomb but slower 'cause it's really big.*

R: Is the Sun a star or is a star something else?

I: *It's a star. They're the same but other stars are further away.*

The Moon

R: What shape is the Moon?

I: *It's like a sphere and it's got a very small pull on the Earth which controls the tides …
but don't ask me how it does this 'cause I don't know.*

R: Is there a shape here that's most like the Moon [selection provided]?

I: *That one. [Picks a sphere.]*

R: How do people know it's that shape?

I: *Because they've been to the Moon.*

R: Can you draw a picture of what you think the Moon would look like from space?
[Draws a circle with 'seas' and 'craters' and a curved terminator.]

R: What colour would it be?

I: *Grey.*

R: Does anything live on the Moon?

I: *No. [Explored.] When spacemen go up and build something they might. You can jump
six times higher on the Moon than on the Earth. There's no atmosphere there … the
Moon's gravity is a lot weaker than the Earth's … about six or seven times less. The
Moon's moving away from the Earth at three centimetres per year.*

R: What is the Moon?

I: *It's another rock like the Earth … it orbits the Earth.*

Such findings were not only restricted to boys. Bethan, for example, was 11 years and 2
months old immediately after teaching when her solar system and concept maps
were produced (see Figures 5.2 and 5.3). Like Ian, Bethan was an 'average' child in
every respect (B = Bethan; R = Researcher).

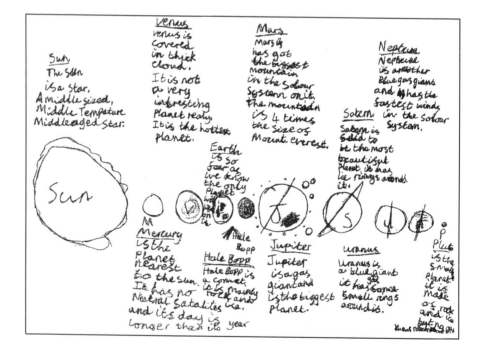

Figure 5.2. Bethan's freehand map of the solar system

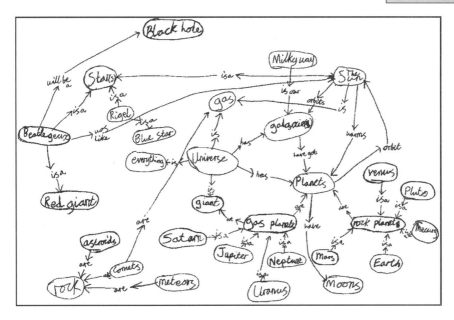

Figure 5.3. Bethan's concept map of the solar system and wider universe

Solar system and wider universe

R: Besides the Earth, the Sun, and the Moon, what else is there in space?

B: *Comets, galaxies … lots of things really … meteorites, nebulas, black holes, planets … their moons.* [Explored.] *A black hole is when a certain type of star dies … a nebula is where stars are born … like the Sun. Galaxies are great big masses of stars and planets. Meteorites … lumps of rock and stone. Comets are gas mostly … most of them.*

R: Do you know the names of the planets?

B: *Mercury, Venus, Earth, Mars, Jupiter, Saturn, Uranus, Neptune and Pluto. There might be one beyond that, we don't know.*

R: Can you draw me a 'map' showing where all of these different things are? [Draws a 'map' as shown in Figure 5.2 with some details added later. Planets correctly named and ordered. Relative sizes, colour and surface details good. Rings around major planets. Jupiter shown with spot and moons though Saturn was described as having most. Unsure about absolute sizes other than 'very big'. The Earth was thought to be '12 thousand or something kilometres' across. Distances remembered as 'very far apart!'. Hottest planet Venus ('it's got clouds all around it and it's very hot'), coldest Pluto ('furthest away'). Mercury was known to orbit the Sun in the shortest time and Pluto in the longest.

R: Do the planets stay where they are or do they move?

B: *They move around the Sun.*

R: *How come they go around the Sun like that, why don't they just 'shoot off' into space?*

B: *'Cause the Sun's gravity's pulling them in so it makes them go around the Sun.*

R: *Do they have an age like you and me or have they always been there [Sun and planets]?*

B: *Yes … they've been there a long time.* [Origin explored.] *After the Big Bang a load of old gas and stuff just splodged out and the planets just formed.*

R: *Do you recognise any of the objects in these pictures [Sun, Moon, nine planets shown]?*
       [All 9 planets, the Sun and the Moon correctly identified.]

Bethan's concept map (see Figure 5.3) provided further information about the depth and structure of her knowledge and understanding. Bethan's map is hierarchical with the universe centrally placed assuming an overall importance and dominance. Below this level, her map is reasonably well integrated reflecting her organisation of knowledge and thoughts.

The richness and complexity of findings such as these raise serious questions about what children are actually capable of learning in science, the validity and reliability of National Curriculum assessment and the uses to which this information is put (compare the learning outcomes presented against the requirements in Table 5.2). The evidence-based research findings presented here, and elsewhere, clearly challenge the basis and rationale upon which many of the decisions taken throughout the development and subsequent evolution of astronomy within the National Curriculum for primary science were made. While it is interesting to note the impact of repeated reviews of the National Curriculum for primary science on the status of individual sub-domains such as astronomy, it would, of course, be wrong to suggest that all curriculum areas were affected in such an extreme way.

Pause for thought

Content and presentation

While all versions of the National Curriculum for primary science have specified the content to be taught, this appears to have been done without much consideration of what children might be interested in or even why they should be learning it at all. Black and Harlen (1993) pointed out that while many areas of science satisfy simple as well as more advanced inclusion criteria, 'blanket-coverage' is not at all necessary and that final content choices should do more to promote a more balanced view of the nature of science and scientific enquiry. Of course, there is no reason at all why all four primary and secondary Key Stages of the National Science Curriculum should contain the same content or appear together in the same documentation and look the same in every way. Or is there? What do you think?

Ownership

Taking ownership of the science curriculum and working creatively and innovatively within its tightly regulated framework requires experience, confidence, a certain degree of risk-taking and a considerable amount of curricular expertise (effectively integrated subject knowledge and subject-related pedagogy or pedagogical content knowledge). With this in mind, and following the lead of Osborne and Simon (1996), Millar and Osborne (1998) and Harlen (1998), the following points are raised for consideration.

The National Curriculum for primary science is a minimum statutory entitlement

As a minimum statutory entitlement, teachers are perfectly at liberty to extend and enhance the science prescribed in statutory documentation as appropriate (content and skills). By including astronomy as nature studies in Key Stage 1 and the solar system and wider universe in Key Stage 2, for example, a better sequential structure for effective teaching and learning and progression between Key Stages is ensured and opportunities to lift and add interest to an otherwise dry minimum entitlement are provided. Cross-curricular support is also essential.

The integration of content and process is far from satisfactory

While AT1 and, now, Sc1 have always been presented as discrete elements in all curriculum versions, the skills, processes and methods associated with scientific enquiry were never intended to be taught in isolation. This lack of integration has simply served to prolong the content vs process debate which has 'plagued' primary science for decades. With astronomy, for example, many teachers initially considered it unsuitable in the primary age phase for it did not conform to their view of the 'hands-on', practical nature of primary science. But this depends entirely on how you perceive and present what 'hands-on' and practical actually mean. Scientists learn in all kinds of ways and children should learn similarly. With this in mind, for example, there is more to the Moon than just its phases: observational drawings (even with care through binoculars or a telescope during the day) provide a starting point for locating, identifying and naming its major features using Moon maps; crater formation can be investigated by way of experimentation and fair testing; using books and other information sources including ICT can be used to review the Moon landings; and the impact of myths and legends associated with the Moon on our society and cultural development can be considered.

Science teaching requires time for the discussion of key issues and other matters

In order to extend scientific ideas and make science more coherent and memorable it has been suggested that scientific knowledge could be presented in the curriculum as a number of key 'explanatory stories' encompassing the 'big' ideas of science. As a result of the narratives involved, it is said, science becomes more alive and children can come to terms with how the 'parts' of their learning form part of a larger framework or 'whole'. Within astronomy, for example, such stories, including those associated with the shape of the Earth, the discovery and motions of the planets and how space is explored, are plentiful. Such stories could also provide essential opportunities to capitalise on the social, affective, emotional and spiritual dimensions of science learning.

Assessment is about more than just factual recall

The assessment framework and testing arrangements for primary science remain steeped in controversy and simply serve to highlight the continued challenges faced when trying to prescribe learning outcomes in detail. To simply know that the Earth, the Sun and the Moon are spherical or near-spherical objects, for example, important though this is, excludes a whole range of other important attributes including what they look like from space, their relative size and their very nature. As observed in the responses provided by Ian and Bethan, thinking and reasoning skills are also sadly neglected.

The science curriculum:

a summary of key points

A National Curriculum of subjects introduced to all maintained schools in England and Wales in 1989 brought compulsory science education into the primary sector for the first time. As a direct result of its elevated profile and an immense amount of hard work and effort by teachers and other professionals responding to requirements, primary science education benefited enormously. Since 1989, however, the development of primary science, and some content areas more than others, has proceeded in a far from rigorous, intellectual and educational manner and without any real acknowledgement of the evidence-based research available to inform it. Many commonly expressed curriculum questions remained unanswered. While there seems little doubt that the introduction of a National Science Curriculum has elevated the profile and changed the very nature of primary science in schools, whether or not the 'best' or the 'right kind' of science is being promoted and taught remains to be seen.

Introduction

Children's natural interest in themselves and the living things around them can make life processes and living things a stimulating and rewarding area of primary science to teach. The wealth of material and resources available provide rich possibilities for learning. Of course, life processes and living things encompasses biology, botany, zoology, ecology, microbiology, genetics, medicine, biochemistry, sustainability and biotechnology. It is important that children at primary school are introduced to these exciting ideas in such a way that the foundations for future learning are laid. In this chapter, some key ideas relating to life processes and living things are discussed and exemplified. Classroom examples are presented in the context of research evidence about how children interact with the living world and the implications for practice are considered.

Learning about life processes and living things

Life processes and living things is considered to be one of the more accessible aspects of primary science and teachers' subject knowledge is often thought to be better in this area than anywhere else. Children, however, often present ideas that are very different to those of the scientific community as a whole. Restructuring children's alternative conceptual frameworks is not an easy task because the ideas held are based upon reasoning that makes perfect sense to them. To help restructure their ideas, it is important that teaching enables children to make progress appropriate to their age and level of attainment. Some conceptual changes may take several years.

What does it mean to be alive?

All living organisms carry out certain processes in order to stay alive. These include, movement, respiration, sensitivity, growth, reproduction, excretion and nutrition. More complex factors such as dormancy, embryology, metamorphosis or dependency on energy transformations are rarely considered (Shepardson, 2002). Some of these ideas are more difficult to understand than others. While younger children often consider whether something is alive or not simply in terms of the more obvious processes such as movement and growth, older children often use a combination of features including external and internal structure, physiological functions and behaviour (Osborne *et al.*, 1992). Tamir *et al.* (1981) also found that children from agricultural backgrounds were more likely to state that seeds and eggs are alive indicating that an individual's personal and direct experiences can be important. Finding out what children know about 'being alive' may be difficult to ascertain for several reasons:

- the concept is complex and the sophistication of children's ideas may be underestimated;
- care is needed to elicit understanding rather than recall;
- different research methodologies may promote different responses.

Pause for thought

Understanding the meaning of 'life' and 'living'

The distinction between 'living' and 'non-living' is not easy for children to assimilate. Children often think that inanimate objects such as clocks, cars and fires are alive and ascribe the attributes of living things to them. Piaget called this animism. Why would children think that these things are alive?

Classification of living organisms

A knowledge and understanding of the classification of plants and animals is important to help children make sense of the world in which they live. It can act as a precursor to introducing more sophisticated classification systems and the more advanced biological concepts of variation and biodiversity. However, children do have difficulty in recognising certain plants as plants and animals as animals. Even during the later stages of schooling, for example, children seem to rely upon physical characteristics such as size and shape when making judgements and have problems classifying living organisms into major taxonomic groups. It may seem reasonable to doubt the value of spending time classifying living organisms per se, and a more useful way to proceed might be to allow children access to as wide a variety of organisms as possible, thus allowing classification skills to be acquired by way of familiarisation. However, this can be risky as learning 'by osmosis' may not necessarily take place effectively. Nevertheless, if classification is learnt in context (e.g. during fieldwork) then not only will the desired outcome be more likely to occur but it will also have more meaning for the child (Tunnicliffe and Reiss, 2000).

Pause for thought

Classifying and identifying plants and animals

Research has shown that a child's ability to identify plants and animals is frequently based upon gross and external physical features. Children therefore find unusual or unfamiliar plants and animals difficult to classify. What generic key skills could children develop as a result of classifying plants and animals? Why is classification important anyway? How can other biological concepts be incorporated into this work? What other scientific knowledge can be acquired as a result of learning about plants and animals?

What is an animal?

Young children tend to base their classification of animals on anatomical features such as shape, size, having four legs, colour and body disrupters such as a trunk (Braund, 1998; Tunnicliffe and Reiss, 1999a). Some studies have shown that older children also have a restricted idea of what an animal is by commonly relying upon a knowledge of pets and things that live on a farm or in a zoo and applying this to the common vertebrate groups only (Trowbridge and Mintzes, 1985). Shepardson (2002) revealed a similar pattern in the development of children's ideas about insects. External physical characteristics such as size and shape were employed for identification purposes and children younger than about 7 years of age used a conceptual framework based upon perceptual and behavioural features (e.g. identifying meal worms as earthworms). Older children provided more complex reasoning based upon more reliable insect characteristics (e.g. having six legs and three distinct body parts) indicating a growing development of biological understanding and morphology in their ability to use accepted taxonomies. Some problems clearly are connected with the use of language. It cannot be assumed that even commonly used words such as 'animal' have the same meaning for the child and the teacher. Children are aware of the everyday usage of the term 'animal' in expressions like 'behaving like an animal' or 'no animals allowed'. The difficulties children experience in developing an understanding of what an animal is can be exacerbated by parlance and the need to take care in language usage. The explanation of specific terms is of prime importance.

What is a plant?

Children's ideas about plants are often restricted to flowering plants (Tunnicliffe, 2001). Children also use systems that are unconventional to classify plants and their ideas are based upon everyday experience and observations as well as everyday language. They recognise and classify plants according to particular external characteristics, including distinctive leaves and colour, and use previous mental models that employ predominantly anatomical features (Tunnicliffe and Reiss, 2000). Some children will group plants according to habitat and older children are more inclined to use recognised taxonomies. Osborne and Freyberg (1985) found that children between 8 and 9 years of age only consider a tree to be a plant when it is young and small. Cabbages, carrots and the like are often classified as vegetables rather than plants and other everyday terms such as weeds and seeds are also put into separate groupings. Making good use of available resources beyond the classroom and observing plants in their natural surroundings will benefit children's ability to identify plants and develop an understanding of the variety of plant life.

According to Warwick and Sparks-Linfield (1996), children tend to consider plants from an anthropocentric viewpoint (e.g. plants exist to provide us with food, to look pretty, or are a nuisance such as weeds in the garden) and remain unaware of their importance relative to animals. They quickly disregard plants as part of the background 'wallpaper' to their world (Schneekloth, 1989; Wandersee and Shussler, 2001). Several influences may contribute to this perception. Plants, for example, do not move about like animals and therefore may not be noticed so readily, plants do not represent such an obvious danger to humans, and plants are not featured in young children's fiction, television programmes or cartoons as frequently as animals.

However, plants form the interface between the physical and biological world in their ability to convert inorganic matter into organic materials through photosynthesis and other metabolic processes. Giving children an insight into understanding what plants are and making them aware of their variety and their physiological processes is vital for a complete understanding of life processes and living things. Plants cannot be overlooked and their importance within ecosystems should be emphasised.

When looking at the germination and growth of plants, children do not clearly understand what is inside a seed or how the process of germination gets underway (Tamir et al. 1981; Russell and Watt, 1990; Jewell, 2002). Germination and the subsequent growth of a plant is seen as a process of unfolding and associated with the appearance of leaves rather than a root and a shoot. Water is often considered to be the most essential requirement for germination to occur. Many children think that a seed contains all that is required for a complete adult plant and very few children consider that new material is incorporated into the plant as it grows. Russell and Watt (1990) found that many primary children considered growth merely as an increase in height, length or volume (in the same way a balloon gets bigger when it is blown up). This 'geometric' perspective indicates a lack of understanding of plant nutrition, transformation, cell division or increase in mass. While younger children often regard the Sun as essential for plant growth, older children cite light together with water, soil and warmth more frequently.

It is not surprising that children find the ideas involved in plant nutrition difficult to understand. The process of photosynthesis cannot be directly observed and for primary children photosynthesis is an extremely abstract concept. As Barker (1995) point out:

> ... the notion that in plant leaves a colourless gas in tiny concentrations in the air, together with ordinary water which we drink, are used to produce a heavy, brown solid and oxygen has the makings of a fairy story.

Indeed children regularly think that 'plant food' is absorbed directly from the soil through the roots rather than, say, manufactured in leaves (Barker, 1995). Comparisons with animal nutrition make this idea of absorbing food from the external environment much more intuitively appealing while the use of 'plant food' and the idea of 'feeding the plants' in everyday experience can understandably support some of these alternative ideas (Barker and Carr, 1989).

Pause for thought

Teaching plant nutrition

Barker and Carr (1989) suggest that referring to the glucose produced in photosynthesis as 'plant product' rather than 'plant food' may help children understand plant nutrition as it removes the notion of plant food as absorbed material and removes analogies with animal nutrition. What does the word photosynthesis actually mean? Does teaching about photosynthesis matter at primary school? Could you teach plant nutrition effectively without reference to the term photosynthesis?

The structure and function of living things

Anatomy and physiology are inextricably linked and the relationship between structure and function is one of the basic tenets of biology. Children's understanding of anatomy is relatively well developed compared to their understanding of the functioning of organs and organ systems (Cuthbert, 2000; Jewell, 2002; Reiss *et al.*, 2002). The emphasis within the National Science Curriculum (DfEE/QCA, 1999) and traditional approaches to biology of 'part naming' and concentrating on labelling anatomical features of living organisms may be a contributory factor that has exacerbated this situation. Although it is important to know correct anatomical terms, relating structure to function while employing correct terminology can facilitate a deeper understanding which will lay valuable foundations for work at later stages in the children's school career and beyond. Children can gain useful and appropriate knowledge by focusing on:

- **the function of an anatomical structure;**
- **why an anatomical structure is the shape and size it is;**
- **what an anatomical structure is made up of and why this is an appropriate material for the function it performs;**
- **how analogous structures differ in a range of organisms;**
- **what homologous features different organisms possess.**

Through the teaching and learning process children can be encouraged to:

- **experience as a wide a range of organisms as possible;**
- **experience real examples, models or virtual examples of the anatomical features being studied;**
- **handle examples of different tissues;**
- **explore, where appropriate, the anatomical features of their own bodies;**
- **compare and describe different homologous and analogous features (e.g. the feet of different mammals, wings and arms);**
- **use correct terminology in context.**

Invertebrate animals

The observational drawing of invertebrates is a popular activity in primary classrooms and can help children to develop an understanding of the anatomy and physiology of the organisms they study as well as refine their observational skills. Observational drawing should be undertaken with care.

As part of some work on 'minibeasts', for example, children in a Year 2 class were studying a tank of snails. The teacher asked them to observe the snails closely and provided the children with hand lenses to facilitate their observations. She proceeded to tell the children the terms for the various anatomical features they had seen. These terms were put onto a board for the children to refer to. The children were asked to draw a snail as carefully and as accurately as possible and label as many parts as they could. Sam, aged 6, had listened very carefully to the teacher and carried out the task (Figure 6.1). However, after Sam had completed his drawing and labelled it, he found that he hadn't used the term 'muscular foot'. This was added later in a rather cartoon-like manner without further observation of the snail. This example helps to demonstrate that:

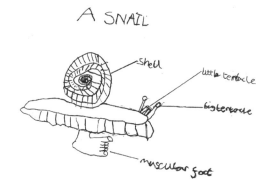

Figure 6.1. Sam's drawing of a snail

- **children will interpret what a teacher says quite literally and in their own way attempt to make sense of it;**
- **children will consider that a teacher is right and employ a term even though the feature has not been observed;**
- **the overemphasis on naming parts may obscure a child's own observations and limit what they draw.**

Vertebrate animals

Reiss *et al.* (2002) suggest that children can have a fairly good knowledge of what is inside their own bodies and can place many of the organs relatively correctly. Children may think that the organs are smaller than they are in reality, especially if they offer no sensation (e.g. the liver or the kidneys). Those that do (e.g. the heart) are usually drawn proportionally larger (Cuthbert, 2000). The drawings that children produce often indicate that spaces exist between organs that are filled with 'blood', 'air' or 'nothing' at all. The notion that the circulatory system is open and that the spaces between organs might be filled with blood persists even into the later school years (Sungur *et al.*, 2001). Blood vessels are frequently drawn as unconnected lines and almost always labelled as veins. While knowledge of individual organs is often relatively good, an understanding of complete organ systems and their function as an integrated whole seems to be limited (Osborne *et al.*, 1992; Tunnicliffe and Reiss, 1999b). The circulatory, muscular and endocrine systems are usually less well represented in drawings than others, although the heart as an individual organ is nearly always shown (though not surprisingly) as a 'valentine' heart which is how it appears on cards and in cartoons. Drawings of the body's internal organs often show a naive respiratory system and an unconnected skeleton. Interestingly, illness often increases knowledge in certain areas. For example, Jim, aged 9, had just returned to school after having had mumps. The impact of mumps on his various glands is there for all to see (Figure 6. 2)! This may be a very appropriate moment to develop ideas about the function of specific systems within the human body.

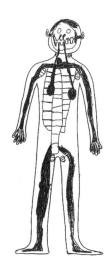

Figure 6.2. Jim's drawing of the body having had mumps

Children often have a relatively good knowledge of the human skeleton and this increases with age (Tunnicliffe and Reiss, 1999b). Braund (1998) ascribes this to familiarity and direct experience initially rather than any teaching in school. However, children tend to represent skeletons as a set of individual and unconnected free floating bones, often stylised as 'dog' bones, indicating that the function of the skeleton, including joints, ligaments and tendons, is not particularly well understood (Cuthbert, 2000). Children's drawings also illustrate this well (Figure 6.3).

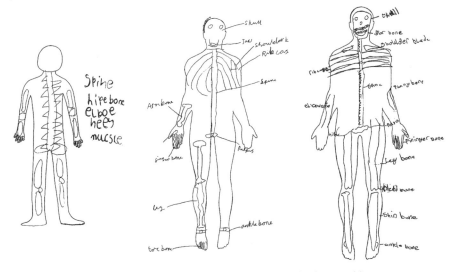

Figure 6.3. Drawings of the human skeleton by 8-year-olds

Knowledge of the skeletal structure of animals other than humans is less well developed. Identification of vertebrates among children is often determined by the presence of distinct features such as an obvious head, limbs and a distinct body outline. Animals such as snakes and fish are not identified as possessing a backbone because they are thought to be too long and thin to accommodate one and that their flexibility would be compromised. Primary aged children tend to overemphasise the curvature and shape of the backbone and this may be due to the fact that they have limited experience of vertebrates other than the human skeletal form as the model for all others. Familiarity with animal movements and their skeletons appears to be important in learning as those children who are more successful in identifying different animals correctly also have direct experience of these animals through visits to zoos or hobbies such as fishing or bird watching. If children are to gain a good understanding of the structure and function of vertebrate skeletons and be encouraged to understand movement and different forms of locomotion, they need to:

- **examine and observe skeletons of different animals;**
- **observe directly the ways different animals move;**
- **look at video material of animals moving and make use of slow-motion clips;**
- **examine X-rays;**
- **make models;**
- **develop fantasy animals and consider how their skeletons might be adapted to particular conditions.**

Pause for thought

The structure and function of living organisms

Understanding the anatomy of living organisms is useful for it can help children to distinguish between different plants and animals and therefore help to classify them. It can also help children understand about life processes (e.g. methods of gaseous exchange, movement in vertebrates, invertebrates, plants, and so on). How can organs and organ systems in humans and other animals, not forgetting plants, be addressed if an atomistic approach is to be avoided and a holistic view encouraged?

Resources to facilitate knowledge and understanding of living organisms

Familiarisation with a wide range of plants and animals seems to be essential if children are to have a good understanding of the biological concepts associated with life processes and living things. The need to provide experiences such as visits to field centres, zoos and museums, and direct work with plants and animals in the local environment seems to be essential. The use of real animals and plants, or parts of their anatomy, may help to ameliorate some of these issues and will assist in developing knowledge and understanding of physiology if structure and function are taught contemporaneously. Of course, there has been a reduction in children's direct experience of plants and animals as a result of health and safety regulations.

Using real plants and animals

A class of Year 5 children had been studying the human cardiovascular system and many resources were available to them (e.g. plastic models, diagrams and wall charts). They still found the structure and function of the heart difficult to understand. In one lesson they were given some sheep hearts to look at (with due permission, precautions and discussion about respect for living things and items that had once been part of a living animal) and now had the opportunity at first hand to understand its three-dimensional nature. The whole class became totally engrossed in the work and the amazement and wonder were palpable in the room. The children learned a great deal as well as developing some crucial scientific skills and social attitudes.

Secondary sources of information

Diagrams and models are often used to illustrate features of plants and animals that cannot be seen readily by children (e.g. the internal structure of a leaf, the digestive system, the skeleton, the cardiovascular system). They are a useful addition to classroom resources although relatively little research has been done on how children perceive them (Gilbert et al., 1998; Harrison and Treagust, 2000). Cuthbert (2000) actually suggests that the use of models does not seem to effect any changes to well established ideas while wall charts and pictures have even less impact. Tabards with attachable cloth body parts may actually reinforce children's 'floating' organ model. Models and diagrams can be valuable teaching and learning tools but it is important to have a clear discussion about the limitations of the resource being used.

Pause for thought

Resources for effective learning

It is generally not so possible to use parts of real animals in school. Cuthbert (2000) suggests that the use of video material and virtual models is better than using static models. How would you help children to a better understanding of the functioning of specific anatomical features (e.g. the heart and circulatory system)?

Using the environment

Environmental awareness and an understanding of sustainability are important. Most researchers agree that meaningful environmental education is more than simply education *about* the environment, it is education *for* the environment, and this involves developing a sense of responsibility and active participation in resolving environmental problems (Palmer and Neal, 1994). However, there is often a tendency to view and approach environmental or sustainability matters from a negative angle in terms of *what's wrong* and *what needs changing*. Teaching about environmental problems in this way may leave children with a sense of individual powerlessness and a consequent disinterest in environmental issues (Bonnett and Williams, 1998). Empowering children to make a difference by engaging them actively in local issues, helping them to gain knowledge of their local environment and to think critically to solve problems is therefore important and may help to remediate some of the problems that children have when considering environmental issues (Grace and Byrne, 2003).

Finding out what children think about the environment in drawings provides a good starting point (Figure 6.4). As children get older, drawings illustrate changes in thinking that mirror findings about the progression of children's ideas of ecological phenomena (Hellden, 1996). As shown, for example, children living in towns and cities often present an egocentric view of the environment initially, one in which 'home' is the central focus. This may develop into an anthropocentric and idealist view in which the environment is there for the benefit of everyone (note the fields,

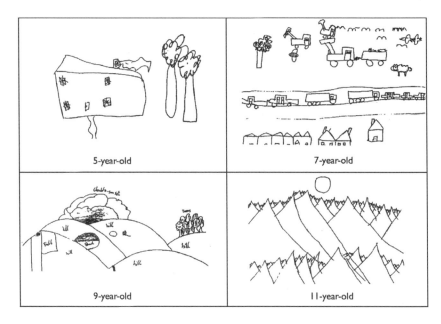

Figure 6.4. The environment

fruit trees, tractors, cottages and birds). Later still, a broader perspective may eventually emerge before the environment becomes almost completely abstract and foreign. Drawings like this fall in line with the findings of Schneekloth (1989) and Wandersee and Shussler (2001) who noted 'blindness' to what the environment contains. It would appear that older children have a notion that the environment is remote from their everyday experience. Perhaps this is not surprising. Children hear and read news items and watch television programmes that talk about the environment and environmental disasters that are usually in distant places. Clearly children need to be given opportunities to work in their local area and investigate the issues that are of concern locally as well as nationally and globally (Grace and Sharp, 2000). Using the local environment has the benefit of being easily accessible and allowing children to study it at regular intervals. This enables them to develop an awareness of what exists in local habitats and how it can change over time, including the factors that influence that change (Egan et al., 2003).

Pause for thought

An awareness of the environment and environmental issues

Research has shown that children may think that environmental issues are not part of their everyday lives and that they cannot do anything about them. This leads to either indifference or a sense of powerlessness. However, environmental work can help children understand many key ideas:

- *there is a very wide variety of living organisms;*
- *plants and animals vary within and between species;*
- *different plants and animals are assigned to specific groups according to how closely related they are;*
- *all living organisms are adapted to survive within particular habitats;*
- *the plants and animals within a habitat/ecosystem are dependent upon each other in a complex and intricate manner;*
- *the Sun is the ultimate source of energy;*
- *plants and animals can survive without human intervention;*
- *food for animals and ourselves does not originate in a pre-packaged form!*

How would you begin to engage interest in environmental issues and to address the key ideas above?

Using the environment gives children excellent opportunities to work beyond the confines of life processes and living things in science to include geography, mathematics, history, personal, social and health education (PSHE) and citizenship. By adopting a cross-curricular approach, ideas such as conservation and sustainability can be made more relevant. Children often thought to underachieve in the classroom are also often found to excel at outdoor activities and research indicates that outdoor education can enhance communication skills, self-esteem and self-confidence (Cooper, 1994). Working with children in the environment develops knowledge, skills, attitudes and values which remain with them long after any work on the environment has come to an end (Eagles and Demare, 1999). A single field trip, however, may be of little lasting value because such experiences have little relevance to children's everyday lives and they are not able to transfer what they have learnt from that experience back to their home settings (Van Matre, 1990). Using the environment does not necessarily mean a special visit to a field study centre, zoo, botanical garden or park, although a special trip can be an exhilarating experience providing valuable additional dimensions to learning, not least the opportunity to see some more unusual plants and animals! However, a great deal of worthwhile and exciting work can be done right on the doorstep of the school, literally in the school grounds or in close proximity to them. The variety of fieldwork that can be undertaken is virtually endless! The question is 'What can be achieved in the time available?' You might like to consider some of the following options:

- observing and noting the variety of plants and animals found;
- classifying the plants and animals found;

- measuring or counting the variety of plants and animals in a given space;
- closely observing the structure and function of different plants and animals;
- considering what eats what (most animals eat a variety of things);
- considering what depends on what (e.g. oaks may depend on squirrels and birds for dispersing acorns);
- considering the human impact on the environment;
- recognising and thinking about what conflicting issues might prevail (e.g. leisure pursuits and conservation);
- developing ideas about safeguarding the environment;
- using games to promote understanding of key principles and concepts.

Environmental work can connect many concepts and themes within life processes and living things (e.g. the notion of energy flow through food chains and webs, competition and interdependence and the important processes involved in the decay of organic matter and cycling of nutrients). These key concepts unify and develop children's conceptual frameworks not only in the biological sciences but they also make strong links to other aspects of science. This contributes to a much more holistic view of the natural and physical world.

Life processes and living things:

a summary of key points

Teaching about life processes and living things is a statutory requirement. But much more than that, it is a fascinating aspect of science that enables children to understand the world they live in to a much greater extent. To encourage children to have a thorough and interconnected understanding of this part of the curriculum the teacher needs to think carefully about what they want the children to learn, choosing interesting and challenging resources, making good use of the local environment including opportunities for first-hand experiences, and opportunities to visit parks, museums, zoos, and so on. Allowing children to appreciate, and have experience of, a wide range of different living organisms and adopting a holistic approach to their anatomy, physiology and interdependence will certainly lay good foundations for work to be undertaken at a later time.

Introduction

Materials constitute the matter from which things are made. Both naturally occurring and manufactured materials exist all around us, yet children's use of the word is often restricted to their immediate and everyday experience. Very early in their lives, young children encounter materials as objects of different sorts with varying properties and know that these can be changed by squeezing them, tearing them, mixing them, and so on. Primary teachers can help encourage children to identify patterns in materials and the way they behave, to raise questions about how they change and the processes of change themselves, to consider cause and effect, and to attempt explanations. In this chapter the development of children's ideas about materials will be considered together with some exploration of the use of the particle model to underpin knowledge and understanding.

Materials and objects

Primary children often focus on the appearance of an object rather than its material composition. Krnel *et al*. (1998), reviewing research related to the development of the concept of matter, proposed that children's knowledge and understanding is influenced by the extent to which they are able to distinguish between matter and objects. To develop understanding, children need to be aware of both the intrinsic properties of a material, which are somewhat independent of the objects they form (e.g. density, hardness, colour), and its extrinsic properties (e.g. mass, volume, size). Through play (e.g. with sand, water, paint, dough), pre-school children develop their awareness of materials from taste, texture, variety and change. When focusing on objects such as a wooden train, for example, it is important to note that the train is made from wood, a material that might be used to make other objects. Russell *et al*. (1991) found that when sorting objects made of different materials, younger children gave greater consideration to surface features than composition whereas older children focused on their possible use. Although material composition is a very important property, it is not always the most discernable or tangible as objects may be painted or coated with other substances.

The term 'made from' can be misleading. When Dickinson (1987) asked a number of children from as young as 4 years of age what a bicycle was made from, half of those involved merely listed individual component parts (e.g. handlebars, seat, pedals, chain). The younger children also had difficulty recognising the material in an object that had been crushed and thought that powdery substances consisted of a different matter from objects made of the same substance. Russell *et al*. (1991) found that almost half of the 5- to 7-year-olds and 9- to 11-year-olds they questioned did not think that it was possible to make metal wool from a metal stick because the stick and the wool have different properties. It is, of course, possible that the children involved may have confused metal wool with sheep's wool in reaching a decision.

Careful observation and the sorting and grouping of objects and materials is a central part of primary science and provides a starting point to help children to make sense of the huge variety of different objects or materials available to them. Work with children in the Foundation Stage provides an important basis to build on. Here it is suggested that children use objects with similar as well as different properties (e.g. size, colour, shape, texture, function) and look at the choice of materials for particular purposes. A common grouping is into natural and manufactured materials. Children may find this difficult where an object is made from a natural material, such as cork, but has been manufactured into an object.

Pause for thought

Important aspects of materials

The world of materials is extensive and constantly expanding. It affects all of our lives. McGuigan (2000) suggests that children's understanding of the origins and transformations of raw materials may be developed by considering processing and visits to small factories or farms. The use of sequenced drawings can provide insights to where objects and materials have come from (Figure 7.1).

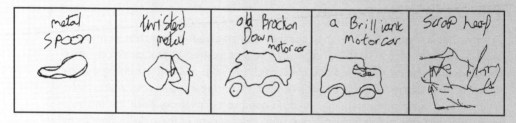

Figure 7.1. Sequenced drawings of the recycling of scrap (from Russell et al., 1991)

What particular aspects of materials do you think are really important for primary children to learn about and why?

Solids, liquids and gases

Grouping materials into solids, liquids and gases helps to understand how they behave. The terms 'solid', 'liquid' and 'gas' can imply that there are sharp distinctions between them but these distinctions are not always so clear. Some everyday materials (e.g. toothpaste, play dough, hair mousse, non-drip paint) are difficult to classify and many (e.g. mousses and foams) are actually mixtures. Weight is an important feature in children's classification of solids, liquids and gases. Powdered solids are often thought to be lighter than lumps and liquids to be lighter than solids. Gases are sometimes described as weightless or even as having 'negative weight', as balloons filled with helium are observed to rise.

Pause for thought

Distinguishing between solids, liquids and gases

Grouping materials into solids, liquids and gases is convenient and the terms are familiar in everyday language. Children's comments on solids, liquids and gases reported by Russell et al. (1991) provide some insight to their ideas:

- *'Flour's a liquid 'cos you can pour it.'*
- *'Liquids are all kinds of things that don't stay where you put them. They just run. If you put them on the table it runs along the table.'*
- *'Air isn't a gas 'cos gas could kill you, but air can't.'*

To what extent do you consider these children to have been able to define the essential features of solids liquids and gases? How might you add to these ideas? How might you go about responding to these ideas?

Children often define solids as hard and strong and find rigid materials or objects with a definite shape the easiest to classify. Squashable or soft materials, such as cotton wool or sponge, or substances with no shape, such as powders and granules, cause some difficulty. Stavy and Stachel (1985) found that only about half of the 5- to 12-year-olds they surveyed were able to classify soft objects and powders correctly as solids. Ice is sometimes not classified as a solid because it can change into water. The broad classification of 'solid' encompasses materials that are too varied to enable children to develop generalising criteria with ease. Children find recognising liquids much more straightforward. Liquids are usually identified, however, as being watery and runny. Some children consider that water is the only liquid that exists while others identify any colourless liquid as water. Viscous liquids that are more difficult than water to pour present some problems, as do coloured or opaque liquids. Many of the liquids children encounter are mixtures involving water (e.g. milk, juice, bubble bath). Although non-aqueous liquids are plentiful (e.g. oil, white spirit, nail varnish remover, alcohol), many of these are not safe for primary aged children to use or should be used only with care and supervision. Children have most difficulty in conceptualising gas as most gases are invisible. Russell *et al.* (1991) indicated that while many children between the ages of 5 and 11 think that there is something called air all around us, relatively few consider air to occupy an empty container. Different gases are often considered as things that can get into the air and spread out. Some children use the term 'gas' more specifically to mean the fuel they encounter in cookers and fires in their homes or to describe something harmful and intangible. They are also likely to call sprays, mists (including steam), flames and smoke gases. The words gas, air and oxygen are often used synonymously. When children talk about water 'turning to air' they may just mean that a gas of some kind is produced.

Implications for teaching about materials

- An understanding of materials may be fostered by using activities in which children can focus on their properties. Playing with natural materials such as sand, stones and water in which shape is not important may help. The use of 'feely-bags' and pieces of material rather than a whole object helps avoid 'object distraction'.

- Teaching should provide not only experiences of solids, liquids and gases but also of the enormous variation within them. Investigation of a wide variety of solids, including powders and granules, and liquids other than water encourages consideration of the properties they have in common and the differences between them. Ranking materials in order according to particular properties may help children understand that these properties are not absolute. The properties of air can be explored by 'feeling' air in bubble wrap, by moving around with open umbrellas or big sheets of cardboard, blowing bubbles and making use of balloons. A range of different gases, including carbon dioxide, helium (in helium balloons), natural gas and oxygen, in addition to air might also be introduced. Weighing full and empty balloons demonstrate that gases, including air, are substances that have mass.

- Models can be introduced to represent particles (e.g. containers of marbles or beads to represent particles in solids, liquids and gases – one full, one half full and the other with just a few in). Freedom or restriction of movement of the marbles when the container is shaken represents the extent of movement of the particles in solids, liquids and gases.

Changes to materials

It is often suggested that by the time children reach primary school they should be aware of materials and how they change over time, change as a result of manipulation (e.g. kneading, and so on), change following mixing, and change after cooking. However, the potential of these experiences may not have been maximised as changes may occur out of sight inside an oven or because cooking is undertaken with helpers who may not be aware of the scope for exploration. Russell et al. (1991) speculated that children's limited familiarity with manufacturing might result from the process being hidden from view and the difficulty of giving children first-hand experience. The role of primary science may be to help develop this awareness and inquisitiveness about the objects children encounter and their production. Teacher confidence and understanding of changes to materials is crucial if experiences are to be explored effectively.

Changes of state

Children may be familiar with some changes of state such as melting (e.g. ice lollies) and evaporation (e.g. socks drying). These are physical changes resulting from the transfer of energy to or from a substance and no new materials are formed. These changes are generally easy to reverse though the product will not necessarily look exactly the same as it did before. Melted wax solidifies when cooled, for example, but unless it is moulded its shape will be very different. Primary teachers can help develop children's understanding of changes of state between solids, liquids and gases and how these changes might be effected. Language use relating to changes of state requires careful consideration. Words such as melting may be used as labels or explanations in themselves without necessarily indicating any particular understanding of the process. Children will also have their own understanding of these words. A single term such as 'evaporation' is a description of a process that occurs in many apparently different situations.

Melting

Energy is required for melting and different materials melt at different temperatures. Krnel *et al.* (1998) refer to research findings that although children might be able to identify melting in ice and understand the change from solid to liquid for water, they are unable to generalise this change from solid to liquid to include other substances. Some children consider that melting always involves water and that melting materials such as wax or butter produces water. They may also think a solid gets lighter when it melts. Hatzinikita and Kouladais (1997) found that many 11-year-olds consider that weight increases when liquid changes to solid. Possibly they think that solid substances stick together better and are consequently heavier. Even where children refer to particles to explain melting, they may describe the particles by using a model in which the particles themselves are thought to melt.

Evaporation

Krnel *et al.* (1998) and Johnson (1998b) stress that evaporation is a processes that is likely to be difficult for children to understand as it involves gases which they find difficult to conceptualise. Evaporation is a complex idea:

- **it involves the apparent disappearance of a liquid;**
- **it occurs in quite different situations varying from a puddle or bowl of water, where the amount of liquid obviously decreases, to clothes drying, or even to those where there is no obvious liquid at all to start with, such as bread drying out;**
- **it may involve a solvent evaporating from a solution to leave a solid residue;**
- **it may also involve liquids such as petrol that are very different to water.**

Bar and Galili (1994) identified four stages in children's understanding of evaporation of water: it disappears; it is absorbed into surfaces; it is transferred upwards to the sky and disperses into air; and it is associated with a change of state. Tytler (2000) developed this progression to include the range of associations children might draw on to support their thinking (e.g. foggy days, steam rising off clothes). Water vapour is difficult for children to imagine. Some consider it to be invisible water particles, some a mixture of water and air and others consider that water has been turned to air. This may result from use of the word 'air' to mean gas or possibly that all gases are air. Explanations rarely involve water changing into vapour that is dispersed in the air around them.

Boiling

Children may be familiar with water boiling in a kettle or saucepan. During boiling, large bubbles of vapour form continuously throughout the liquid and rise to the surface from where the vapour enters the surrounding environment. For boiling to start and to be maintained, a continual input of energy is required. The most obvious signs of change include the formation of bubbles and visible steam. The loss of liquid from the kettle or saucepan is less obvious and even where this is noticed the link between loss of liquid and formation of vapour bubbles is rarely made. Osborne and Cosgrove (1983) asked 8- to 18-year-olds about the bubbles in boiling water. Responses indicated that that they might consist of heat, air, oxygen, hydrogen or steam. Most identified the visible mist coming away from boiling water as 'steam', probably drawing on the common use of the word to describe water vapour, which has cooled slightly and condensed as small droplets of liquid water, rather than water in the truly gaseous state. Some considered that the water had become air. A detailed study including 11-year-olds led Johnson (1998b) to conclude that while children are aware that water somehow leaves boiling water as a mist (which then disappears), any connection with the bubbles is in doubt. Johnson also suggested that Bar and Travis (1991) were somewhat too optimistic in their assertion that children understand that during boiling liquid is changed into gas. The change from liquid to gas is not well understood and the meanings of 'steam' and 'air' are problematic. Children's responses should be further explored where possible. However, it is unlikely that primary children will understand or accept that the bubbles in boiling water are water as a gas. This is a further indication that children find the gaseous state to be somewhat mysterious and that the idea of a gas being a sample of a substance just as an iron nail or a pool of water is by no means an obvious one. Most of the 11-year-olds in Johnson's study did not start with the idea that water could exist as a gas – informing children that bubbles in boiling water are water in the gas state is not enough to persuade them! He suggests that children need a means of seeing why such a happening is a possibility and that the idea of particles used appropriately may help to develop this. Looking at boiling may be helpful in establishing the foundation that water can become a gas – this may later be built on further to develop the idea of other gases each of which are different substances.

Condensation

Condensation is perhaps the most difficult of all the physical changes to understand as it involves the appearance of a liquid from invisible vapour. During condensation energy is transferred from gaseous substances producing particles with less vigorous movement which become more closely packed and result in the formation of a liquid. Few children are able to accept that there is water vapour in the air or that water vapour could change into liquid water. They find the formation of condensation on cold surfaces difficult to explain and may believe that it is formed as a result of displacement (i.e. the water that was on the inside of the container has moved to the outside to form the water droplets on the cold surface). They may consider it involves coldness changing to water or that it is the result of hot meeting cold (Tytler, 2000).

Concept cartoons (Keogh and Naylor, 1997; Naylor and Keogh, 2000) are useful for finding out about children's ideas in science and for initiating discussion and investigation. Children are generally motivated to discuss the opinions of the characters in the cartoons and this is valuable for challenging and developing their ideas. Kruger and Summers (1989) and Harlen and Holroyd (1997) have indicated the difficulties teachers experience explaining changes of state including condensation and concept cartoons can also be used to develop curricular expertise. A group of graduate trainee teachers were asked to consider the concept cartoon shown in Figure 7.2. Responses mainly agreed with the statement '*I think the vapour in the air has turned into drops of water on the glass*' but their explanations indicated some uncertainty about what happens during condensation:

What do YOU think?

Figure 7.2. Children's ideas about condensation (from Naylor and Keogh, 2000)

'... think that the ice cubes and perhaps heat play a part somewhere but not sure';
'... because water is contained in the air and a chemical change occurs when the air comes in contact with the cold surface and turns to water';
'... as the air touches the glass it cools. As it cools the gas condenses. The hydrogen and oxygen combine to create drops of water'.

Jarvis *et al.* (2002) made use of a concept cartoon involving an ice cream tub and asked a group of graduate trainee teachers to explain as carefully as they could why the outside of the tub was wet. As well as showing all of the ideas indicated in the cartoon bubbles some explanations demonstrated considerable confusion:

'... because the change in temperature and the water is produced through condensation breaking down the molecules (dissolving)!'

Trainees' explanations after a taught session and peer discussion were scrutinised to look at their use of ideas of particles and energy compared to those given before. Increased use of both particles and energy in responses was evident:

'... the water has come from the air – as the air hits the cold container the water vapour condenses into a liquid' (*pre-*);

'... the water vapour in the air of the room comes into contact with the colder container. Heat is lost causing the water vapour particles to lose energy and slow down. After a point condensation: the change of state from gas to liquid, occurs and the water particles are visible as liquid' (*post-*).

Some responses that demonstrated greater use of particles and energy still implied the water was produced when air, rather than water vapour, was cooled on the cold surface.

Pause for thought

Changes of state

Changes of state are usually the result of energy transfers. Can you explain why a drop of surgical spirit on your hand feels colder than a similar drop of water? Why do clothes dry faster on a warm windy day? Where does the heat energy go when candle wax solidifies?

Implications for teaching about changes of state

- Opportunities should be provided for showing a variety of materials changing state under different conditions and in different contexts. Similarities and differences in the behaviour of different materials should be explored through melting and evaporation. ICT can be used to support this with examples not available in the classroom.

- Children may have difficulty accepting the idea of reversibility of melting as the starting material may look different before and after heating. Exploration of reversibility by melting ice, chocolate or wax and then solidifying it again in moulds allows the construction of stories of the production of objects. This can be developed to include a wider range of examples involving change of state such as melting metals which cannot be done practically.

- Weighing material during changes such as those described above can help to illustrate conservation of matter and mass. Changes involving gases are more problematic but can be demonstrated by collecting condensed water vapour from evaporation or boiling. Careful observation of boiling with a focus on both the bubbles and loss of water may help.

- Comparison of materials melting at different temperatures (e.g. ice, wax) provides opportunities for confident teachers to employ the particle model and consideration of the role of heat energy in melting to explain the similarities and differences in behaviour. Pendlington et al. (1993) identified a series of activities for teachers to consider the use of particles to explore change of state. Modelling particles in solids, liquids and gases may help children visualise change of state even when they are unsure of the nature of the substances involved (Johnson, 1998a).

- Although both adults and children use words relating to change of state (e.g. melting, evaporation) confidently they do not necessarily understand the process involved or share the scientific meaning of the words. This is well illustrated in the water cycle which involves ideas of both evaporation and condensation. Many children can accurately label a standard water cycle diagram but this does not mean that they understand either the water cycle or the processes involved in it. Some children, for example, consider that the water cycle can only happen at the coast. When the water cycle is being taught, care should be taken to explore children's ideas of the changes of state within the cycle possibly by asking them questions which require explanation rather than just recall. For instance, ask them to consider whether the processes of evaporation and condensation are reversible or why rain isn't salty yet seawater is.

Dissolving

Dissolving describes one possible change initiated by mixing. This involves the formation of such an intimate mixture that the resulting solution may show no sign of the dissolved material at all. The original solute can, however, be recovered from solution and the mixture separated. Dissolving is a reversible process. Reversible and irreversible changes are often considered synonymous with physical and chemical changes. Oversby (2000) argues that this is not necessarily the case pointing out that some physical changes (e.g. breaking or cutting) are clearly irreversible. That said, salt can be retrieved from a salt and water solution so dissolving is a reversible change. However, this requires some care – just as when a £5 note is deposited in a bank, withdrawal of a £5 note does not produce the same note that was deposited. The recovered salt particles will be in different positions in the crystal and in practice it is extremely unlikely that exactly the same number of crystals will be reproduced.

Although dissolving may involve solids, liquids and gases, children's experience of dissolving is most likely to be limited to sugar and salt mixed with water. Young children often describe the solid as 'disappearing' when it dissolves. Their use of the word disappearing may reflect different meanings. It may mean the solid can no longer be seen, it may suggest that the solid has actually gone, or it may be a response acknowledging what has been seen with a lack of certainty about what has happened (Hatzinikita and Koulaidis, 1997). Longdon et al. (1991) suggested that the use of materials such as sugar and salt which produce colourless solutions might reinforce the idea that a solid disappears. Alternatively children may observe that when sugar or salt is added to water it 'melts' away. Again this may be descriptive but some children do consider melting and dissolving to be very similar (Stavey and Stachel, 1985; Driver, 1985). Children's confusion may result from a focus on the fate of a solid which goes 'runny' while ignoring the role of water in dissolving and not recognising that melting is related to a particular temperature. Use of hot water appears to reinforce ideas about melting. Selley (2000) interprets this as children focusing on what is similar rather than looking for differences. Blanco and Prieto (1997) report that some children regard stirring as an essential prerequisite for dissolving. Even though some children describe sugar and salt as disappearing when they dissolve, they are often aware that the solution tastes sweet or salty. This indicates some idea of the conservation of matter during dissolving. It is possible, however, that the taste is thought to be a component of the solute rather than being an intrinsic part of it. Hatzinikita and Koulaidis (1997) recommend that issues of conservation of matter and mass be considered separately. Even where children accept that the solute is still present in the solution (conservation of matter) they may consider that the effect of the water is to make the solid lighter so that the material in the final solution weighs less than the sum of the components (no conservation of mass). They think the solid is absorbed, or supported, by the liquid, or that liquids are lighter than solids. Children may refer to dissolving being a reaction between water and sugar. This may be an indication of a chemical change rather than a physical change.

Research indicates that few children are able to explain dissolving in terms of particles (Krnel et al., 1998). However, those that do use particles to explain dissolving tend to describe the sugar or salt as slipping into spaces between the water particles. Sometimes they describe the water as pushing apart the sugar or salt particles and explanations can be mechanistic describing large pieces being crushed into smaller pieces or big particles breaking to give smaller ones. Holding (1987), in a cross age study involving children as young as 8 years of age, found that use of particles of solute increased steadily with age but that representation of the solvent particles was rare. Jarvis et al. (2003) found that a group of primary teachers demonstrated confusion between melting and dissolving. Although particles were referred to in a number of cases, the understanding behind the term was often incomplete, ambiguous or confused, with diagrams showing the distribution of sugar and salt particles among the water but without any indication that the water is made up of particles.

Children have little experience of gases dissolving although they are very familiar with fizzy drinks. Carbon dioxide gas and water can be mixed easily and effectively using a Soda Stream. The gas can easily be separated from the mixture so it is possible to explore the idea of reversibility of dissolving and the amount of gas in a bottle of drink. Fizzy drinks also provide an opportunity for consideration of conservation of matter and mass. Concept cartoons can be used to encourage children to discuss, predict and investigate conservation of mass (Figure 7.3). A group of graduate teacher trainees were given this problem to consider at the start of a support session focusing on the idea of particles (Jarvis et al., 2002). While most gave a correct response, less than half of those involved were able to offer a satisfactory explanation. Some responses recognised that the container was losing gas bubbles but indicated a view that gases have no mass:

'… container [of lemonade] will stay the same because the bubbles had no weight in the first place'.

Such responses indicated the need for support if new teachers are to be able to teach science effectively.

What do YOU think?

Figure 7.3. Children's ideas about gases (from Naylor and Keogh, 2000)

Implications for teaching about dissolving

- Mixing and separating a wide variety of solids, liquids and gases will provide opportunities for considering the nature of the mixtures and any changes that occur. Oversby (2000) suggests broadening the range of materials used for dissolving to include coloured ones. Longdon et al. (1991) indicated that children may have difficulty considering dissolving when it involves dissolving something out of something else (e.g. tea from tea leaves). When these examples are used, care should be taken to explore the dissolving process focusing on conservation of the solute using sight, taste, and weighing the solute and solvent prior to mixing and again after mixing.

• Active use of the particle model, physical models and analogies may all be helpful to explore dissolving. A physical model for dissolving might involve mixing dried lentils and sultanas. The lentils represent the water particles with little space between them. When the sultanas are added there is a simple mixing of the two. Children can be asked to act as particles of solids and water to explore solubility. Oversby (2000) provides a helpful analogy for the process of dissolving sugar in water with children at the dinner counter – only those at the counter can get served and the others must wait their turn. He points out the limitation of the model by acknowledging that, of course, sugar can dissolve from all over its surface whereas the children can only be served a few at a time. Children can be encouraged to develop and evaluate their own analogies and to increase their awareness of the limitations of all models and analogies.

Chemical change

The everyday use of materials provides insights to a wide variety of chemical changes (e.g. cooking, burning, decay, rusting, and so on). Chemical changes result in new materials being formed, may involve changes of energy or colour, and are generally hard to reverse. Both heating and mixing may result in chemical change as well as the physical changes considered previously. A particular difficulty for primary science teaching involves children's familiarity with everyday materials, many of which are often quite complex mixtures. These undergo a variety of changes which can appear somewhat mysterious and magical to children.

Pause for thought

Everyday changes

Krnel et al. (1998) indicate that children may describe chemical changes in term of physical processes (e.g. ageing of iron rather than rusting) and confuse chemical reactions with simple mixing. A chemical reaction between two substances may be described as 'mixing' even though there may be a change in something obvious like colour. Children tend to focus on how reactions start and finish rather than on what is happening during them. Making sense of what happens can be difficult. What problems might be encountered in explaining the following everyday occurrences to children?

- *a match lighting;*
- *bath salts fizzing;*
- *a nail rusting;*
- *paper burning.*

A candle burning illustrates some of the difficulties encountered with an everyday process. When Jarvis et al. (2002) asked graduate teacher trainees to explain what was happening, their responses indicated that they were mainly aware of the flame and the wax melting. Some were able to indicate that the wax was melting as a result of heat from the flame, but there appeared to be little understanding of the wax being drawn up the wick and vaporising or of the actual process of burning. Few indicated that burning requires fuel (in this case the wax as well as the wick) and oxygen, that new products were formed, or that the transfer of heat and light energy to the surroundings was the result of the chemical reaction. If fuel was mentioned at all it was often thought to be the wick. Similarly, children may suggest that the water, gases or smoke produced as the result of burning were originally contained in the fuel and were released during combustion. They are likely to be very unsure about the role of oxygen because it plays no obvious part in the burning. The concept of conservation of mass during chemical reactions, especially burning, is parti-cularly difficult as there are gaseous reactants and products and one of the reactants is obviously used up. In this case, products are thought to be lighter than reactants. Johnson (2000) indicated that although many 11-year-olds can correctly identify reac-tions they have little idea of what has happened.

Implications for teaching about chemical change

- **Primary teachers can look at a wide variety of changes, including those that occur over different timescales, and encourage discussion about the signs and causes of change. Some changes result in the obvious production of new products. Those in which gases are produced would provide opportunities to explore further properties of gases such as volume and mass.**
- **Activities of the type detailed by Pendlington et al. (1993) are thought provoking and encourage very close scrutiny of a candle burning by looking at the effect of removing oxygen, exploding the wax vapour near to the flame, and so on. These may help to develop understanding of the candle burning.**

Particle theory

The particle theory of matter provides a powerful model and tool for the explanation and interpretation of the properties and behaviours of different materials. Despite the difficulties that some primary teachers may themselves have in learning about the particle theory of matter (Kruger and Summers, 1989; Harlen and Holroyd, 1997: Jarvis et al., 2003), those confident in its use are able to provide appropriate opportunities for the development of children's ideas. In this model, all matter is thought to consist of small particles (e.g. atoms, molecules, ions). Particles in the solid liquid or gas of any material are the same, just differing in energy, movement and arrangement. Awareness of some of the difficulties presented by the abstract particle model may actually help teachers to review their own ideas and to consider how to work with children. Acting as the particles in solids, liquids and gases may be helpful. Trainee teachers showed a considerable improvement in their use of the parti-cle model and energy to explain changes of state and dissolving having participated in an intensive programme of activities designed to provide strong visual representations (Jarvis et al., 2002). In a three-year study of children as young as 11 years of age, Johnson (1998a) found that some had no awareness of particles at all, or only mentioned particles that they had 'been told' about. Others imagined that particles existed in addition to a substance itself (Figure 7.4). Johnson (1998a) commented further that the routine classification of materials into solids, liquids and gases does little to help the development of children's knowledge and understanding that solids, liquids and gases are interchangeable. Using the particle model may promote the idea that properties depend on state whereas the state depends on the behaviour of particles. Everyday usage of the word 'particle' is also problematic and might suggest a grain or a speck of material. Where particles are seen as the smallest bits of materials, their size and shape may be considered to be determined by the state, with gas particles thought to be small and round, liquid particles irregularly shaped and solid particles large and cubic or cuboid. Children find the idea of 'nothing' between particles difficult to grasp and often suggest that there must be something there especially in gases. This something is often referred to as 'air'. Children show little appreciation of the motion of particles and even fewer have any idea of the force of attraction or cohesion between them.

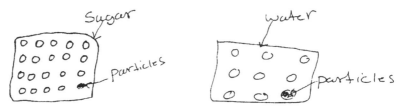

Figure 7.4. Children's drawings of particles (from Johnson, 1998a)

Pause for thought

Thinking about particles

Particles in the solid, liquid or gaseous states of any material are of the same type but differ in their energy, movement and arrangement. This can be used to explain the differences between solids, liquids and gases, and also to illustrate what happens during changes of state, dissolving and so on. How might you use the particle model to explain:

- *why different solids melt at different temperatures?*
- *why increasing the temperature might increase the rate of dissolving?*
- *why the boiling point of water decreases with altitude?*

Implications for teaching about particles

- Johnson (1998a) considered that the different images of particles held by children might represent a progression in children's developing understanding of particle theory and that aspects of teaching might influence the development of these images. The idea of particles within a continuous substance might be reinforced by diagrams of particles within a substance or by phrases such as 'the particles in a solid'. The classification of substances into solids, liquids and gases and reference to the three types of substance and three types of particle may not be particularly helpful in developing children's understanding of change of state. Describing 'the smallest bit of substance' might foster the image of particles as the end product of a lengthy cleavage procedure. As children's ideas of the existence of particles become stronger, the particles then become associated with the substance and its behaviour. The particles can then be thought of as 'being similar' to the substance and eventually 'being' the substance.

- The particle model should be considered carefully by teachers to support their own understanding of matter, especially their ability to consider solids, liquids and gases as states of matter which are interchangeable. Teachers with confidence are able to plan imaginative teaching and learning opportunities in which cross-curricular links are maximised providing opportunities for children to explore scientific ideas in different ways.

Materials:

a summary of key points

Children of all ages have experience of many varied materials. This provides primary teachers with the basis for discussion and investigation of their properties, their uses, their origins and the transformations they undergo. Children's ideas about materials, however, should not be taken for granted. Care needs to be taken with words that have both everyday and scientific meanings and with children who use words such as 'evaporation' or 'condensation' with confidence for this may mask limited understanding. For the primary teacher, the complexity of many everyday materials and the changes they undergo present some challenges, and judicious choices may need to be made to select appropriate examples for particular purposes. Causes of change are important to explore although they are not always immediately obvious. Models should be used and developed as appropriate to support explanation and interpretation.

8 PHYSICAL PROCESSES

GRAHAM PEACOCK AND ROBIN SMITH

Introduction

Children in primary schools are taught about physical processes including electricity, forces and motion, light and sound, and the Earth in space (DfEE/QCA, 1999). In this chapter we focus upon the teaching of electricity and forces. We examine how children's ideas may develop and illustrate a range of teaching strategies applicable to these topics.

The nature of physical processes

The ideas underlying physical processes are felt by many people to constitute a particularly demanding set of concepts for children and reports continually draw attention to the need for effective teaching within this domain (e.g. QCA, 2002). Similarly, studies such as those carried out by Summers and Kruger (1993) and Harlen et al. (1995) suggest that many primary teachers actually find physical processes an area where they feel perhaps most insecure in their own subject knowledge. Indeed, electricity and forces often feature in debates about what should be left until secondary school. Underlying such debates are questions of what knowledge and understanding is desirable and achievable. There are questions about the sorts of scientific explanations and concepts that need to be learnt and also about how far children can engage meaningfully with them. In England, for example, teachers and schools moved in a few years from being reluctant to teach these two topics to adopting them as taken-for-granted in schemes of work. Vickery (1995) noted that when it was suggested to move electricity out of the Key Stage 1 Programmes of Study for science in earlier National Curriculum reviews, overwhelming opposition was voiced from infant teachers who said it should be retained because 'the children enjoy using batteries and bulbs and making them light'. Vickery contrasted two schools of thought about teaching the ideas of electrical circuits:

- **one holds that understanding these is an abstract thing and requires a certain level of development so teaching should be delayed;**
- **the other argues that understanding is rooted in early and repeated exposure to experiences which have the concepts embedded in them.**

Pause for thought

Why should primary children learn about physical processes?

Putting aside current requirements for a moment, reflect on what you think primary schools should teach about electricity and forces and why. The case for their inclusion may be made, for example, on grounds of interest, opportunities for practical activity, relevance to everyday life, scientific literacy, preparation for secondary schooling or the needs of the economy. The case against may be based on the conceptual difficulties involved, the crowded curriculum or the need for teachers to have sufficient subject knowledge.

Electricity

By general consensus, children between the ages of 5 and 7 years of age should be taught about:

- **everyday appliances that use electricity;**
- **simple series circuits involving batteries, wires, bulbs and other components including switches;**
- **the dangers of electricity.**

Building on that, and between the ages of 7 and 11, children should be taught:

- **to construct circuits incorporating a battery or power supply and a wider range of components to make electrical devices work;**
- **how changing the number or type of components in a series circuit can make bulbs brighter or dimmer;**
- **how to represent series circuits by drawings and conventional symbols, and how to construct series circuits on the basis of drawings and diagrams using conventional symbols.**

With the foundations of electricity in place, children can progress through secondary science to know how to design and construct series and parallel circuits and how to measure current and voltage, to know that the current in a series circuit depends on the number of cells and the number and nature of other components and that current is conserved, and to know that energy is transferred from batteries and other sources to other components. Throughout the primary years of schooling, the focus is on electricity flowing around circuits. Schemes of work, such as the *Scheme of Work for Science at Key Stages 1 and 2* commonly adopted by schools (QCA/DfEE, 1998, with amendments 2000), suggest a progression of activities in which children:

- **make simple circuits and draw them;**
- **use drawings to make circuits;**
- **solve problem circuits and make solutions (e.g. to light a house);**
- **test materials in circuits to see which conduct electricity and which do not;**
- **control circuits and apply what they know to models.**

Practical activities such as these are valuable for children's engagement and motivation but practical activity on its own is not enough. Those experiences should be linked with investigation and discussion to promote deeper understanding. Hollins and Whitby (2001) summarise this journey as follows:

> The effects of electricity can be experienced by children at an early age. Wiring up model houses to light them and provide bells can be successful in Year 1. The eventual challenge will be for them to differentiate the material nature of the current (not used up) from the energy transferred to the lamp or bell. This for most children will be in late primary or early secondary school.

To promote growth of understanding, it is important to know what ideas children may have and how to best interact with them.

Ideas about electricity

There have been numerous studies that have focused on children's ideas about electricity including the seminal work of Osborne and Freyberg (1985), and many have been carried out by teachers or by student teachers in their own classrooms and with primary children (e.g. Jabin and Smith, 1994). Not surprisingly, it has been revealed that children's ideas are often incomplete and many hold alternative interpretational frameworks rather than a standard scientific view of what happens when electric current flows around a circuit. *Sink* models, in which current is believed to be consumed by bulbs and by other components in a circuit, are particularly common, as are models where the current flows in two directions from opposite ends of a battery and *clash* when they meet (Figure 8.1).

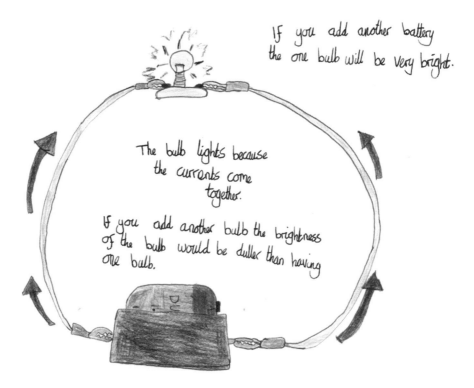

Figure 8.1. Child's drawing of how electricty travels in a circuit (clashing current model)

The research evidence is useful as it indicates what needs to be done when children are taught. Teachers cannot assume that children will start without preconceptions or misconceptions and that their teaching will simply provide an explanation that will be readily accepted and adopted. Although the evidence of alternative views is well established, it only provides teachers with a general indication of what to expect since the range of ideas might be vast. Setting children to make circuits and to apply ideas in new problems may reveal the extent of their knowledge, but it cannot be assumed that making successful circuits is evidence of underlying understanding about how they work. So when they start any teaching on electricity, teachers need to find what ideas children already have. Researchers have used methods which can also be adapted by teachers to elicit children's existing ideas and then to assess their learning in classrooms. These methods include:

- **presenting drawings of circuits and asking children to predict whether they would work;**
- **getting children to draw circuits which they think would work;**
- **interviewing the children about these drawings to explore their explanations for the predictions;**
- **giving children limited equipment to make a circuit and light a bulb;**
- **asking what they expect to happen when other devices are added to circuits, for instance a second identical bulb in series.**

As well as holding general ideas about how electrical circuits work, children may also have particular ideas about the parts of a battery or bulb which can be connected to make it conduct electricity (Parker and Heywood, 1996), about what a battery does and about what happens when it 'runs down'. They may also have images of what happens inside a wire that teachers need to take into account. Kibble (2002) investigated how children and student teachers pictured this (Figure 8.2). The majority produced a *wavy/sparky* picture when asked to draw what they would see if they imagined themselves very small inside a wire. The goal of his subsequent teaching was to shift them toward a model of moving particles (electrons) which was used by secondary pupils.

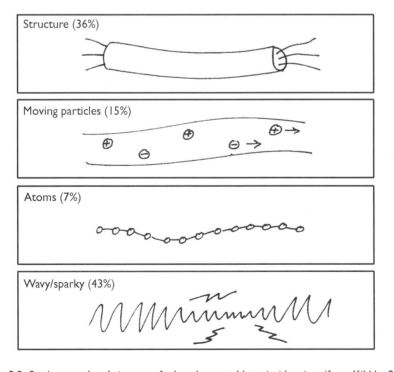

Figure 8.2. Student teachers' pictures of what they would see inside wires (from Kibble, 2002)

Of course adults, including teachers, may hold ideas that are not consistent with the standard scientific account of current flow which in many ways is counter-intuitive. While it is certainly necessary for teachers to have good scientific knowledge, that alone is not sufficient. A teacher's understanding of electricity needs to be closely linked to its use in practice. Daehler and Shinohara (2001) describe how these two aspects of knowledge might be developed in conjunction when cases of teaching are examined by teachers themselves. One example that they gave to groups of teachers to discuss, with the support of a facilitator, was of a dilemma faced by a female teacher when children were presented with a common sequence of challenges: first to find a way of lighting a bulb with a battery and two wires and then using just one wire. Initially, however, many children were convinced that the bulb shown in a drawing to be short-circuited would actually light (Figure 8.3). As they discussed the evidence from children's work and of the teacher's recorded reflections, the groups of teachers involved clarified their own subject knowledge and understanding (such as how the electricity flowed in different types of drawings) and also their own pedagogical reasoning (such as what makes these ideas hard for children). Daehler and Shinohara (2001) concluded that teachers can learn effectively from the use of cases if those interweave several different aspects of the same problem: a closely focused piece of science content; an understanding of what makes that particular science easy or hard for children to learn; considering successful teaching strategies, and considering different ways of representing difficult ideas.

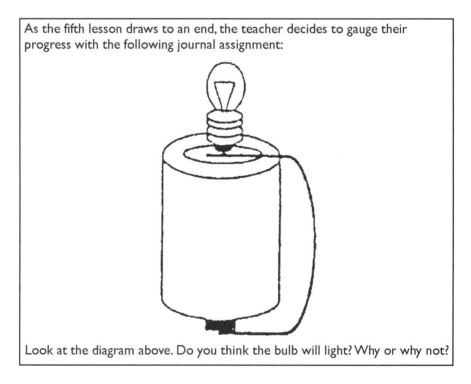

As the fifth lesson draws to an end, the teacher decides to gauge their progress with the following journal assignment:

Look at the diagram above. Do you think the bulb will light? Why or why not?

Figure 8.3. Drawing of short-circuited bulb shown to children
(from Daehler and Shinohara, 2001)

Teaching electricity

Suggestions for teaching electricity in primary schools tend to emphasise practical activities (e.g. examining devices that use batteries, getting children to make and draw simple circuits and to explore circuits that work and do not work, controlling circuits by incorporating switches and other devices). However, some of the reasons why teachers were concerned about teaching electricity when it was introduced to the primary curriculum were to do with resources and management as much as the content. In order to achieve the sorts of lessons recommended, classes need a sufficient supply of reliable equipment and need to be able to participate in effective group work. Experience has shown a number of things which make lessons more successful and less demanding:

- **not assuming that all children have to construct circuits at once as drawing and discussion are also important activities;**
- **maintaining a sufficient supply of a limited range of equipment, standardised on batteries and bulbs of matching voltage;**
- **checking these components are working;**
- **establishing a simple system of storage and retrieval which is part of the school's system for science equipment;**
- **teaching children to use the system responsibly, teaching them skills such as making connections.**

As well as introducing children to circuits and components it is essential to develop their knowledge and understanding of how these work. Constructivist approaches which build on insights into preconceptions and misconceptions emphasise the importance of first eliciting and then challenging children's ideas.

When introducing scientific explanations and asking children to accept those as better accounts of what they observe, the goal is for them to build up a new set of meanings and understandings. The effectiveness of this will depend not just on what ideas they already have but also on how they hold these. This was illustrated in a study on understanding current flow and connections in circuits carried out by Shepardson and Moje (1999) with a class of 8- and 9-year-olds. The children were given 12 simple circuit diagrams. Working in groups they predicted in which the bulb would light before testing their predictions by making the circuits. The teacher then used an analogy of a circus ring to introduce the idea of current travelling in a circular path to the whole class. She drew simple circuits and asked them to predict if a bulb would light in each circuit and to say why. The next day, the groups made simple circuits and drew those which worked, passing their diagrams to another group to check. As a final test, the children were given diagrams of bulbs and batteries on which they were asked to draw in the wire connections. Before and after this sequence of teaching, the researchers also interviewed eight of the children using circuit problems, diagrams and drawing tasks to probe their understanding. Shepardson and Moje found patterns in the ways that different children responded to anomalous data (i.e. when circuits behaved in ways that did not match their predictions and explanations). They reported three sorts of response, each typified by Erin, Zane and Grace.

Erin

Children like Erin who had well-formed but scientifically inaccurate frameworks of ideas about current and connections in circuits amended their ideas in the light of anomalous data because they saw these as conflicting with their observations. Erin's frameworks reflected specific details about battery and bulb connections which she used consistently and coherently in different electric circuit tasks. At the start, she focused on connecting the tip of the bulb to the negative battery terminal and displayed some non-scientific views about current flow. During the teaching sequence her experience of anomalous data and the explanations by other children conflicted with her ideas (E = Erin; B and V are two other children):

V: It's going to light.
B: Agree.
E: It won't.
B: Why do you think it won't light?
E: The wire's not touching the negative part of the battery and tip ... Why do you think it will light?
V: Because it's touching the top of the battery ... the wire touches the bottom of the battery.

[*Children build the circuit and become excited when the bulb lights.*]

E: Wow! It lights!
V: I told you it would.

After the teaching sequence Erin restructured her understanding as a result of the conflict she experienced, apparently helped by the teacher's circus ring analogy:

E: A circuit is like when the bulb [*inaudible*] need two wires for it ... Well you could do with one ... you could just put the [*points to the tip*] light bulb [*points to the negative battery terminal*] right there and ... the wires so it [*electricity*] can just go in a flow [*points to side of bulb and positive battery terminal*].

Zane

However, some children like Zane who had different frameworks were able to accommodate the unexpected observations with little change to their existing ideas. His explanations of connections were not consistent from task to task but he did sometimes draw scientifically accurate connections. The core idea behind Zane's thinking about circuits seemed to be the flow of *power* (using his terminology). This he used to illustrate his clashing currents model:

Z: The power comes out of the top and bottom [*of the battery*] and into the bulb.

Zane's predictions were challenged by only one of the circuit tasks so he was able to modify his ideas about connections slightly but ignore the teacher's explanation of current flow. After teaching he accurately drew connections in two out of three circuits but illustrated a clashing currents model in all three. He showed how his understanding was placed in a well developed, consistent but scientifically inaccurate framework when he explained how 'the pluses and minuses meet in the light bulb and rub together to make electricity'.

Grace

Other children like Grace did not have coherent frameworks of ideas about circuits, nor did they form any as a result of the teaching. This was perhaps because they maintained multiple and inconsistent frameworks throughout and failed to recognise the data as challenging their understandings. Before the teaching Grace showed different ideas when talking about different circuits:

G: No. Yes. Or no. Yes. As long as wire touch the tip of the bulb ... electricity going to light bulb. No. The electricity will go like this [*tracing a clashing current model on the circuit diagram with her finger*] ... [*Pointing to wire*] On side of bulb so won't light. Electricity can't get to the bulb.

Although many of the circuits Grace was faced with challenged her predictions and explanations, she appeared to interpret data from each one in isolation rather than seeing them as pointing to an overall explanatory framework. Although she incorporated additional details into her accounts of circuit connections these remained inconsistent and so did her explanations about electricity flow.

The implications of the study for teaching indicate that children move toward more scientific explanations and understanding but that simply presenting them with data that do not fit their predictions is not always guaranteed to work. Shepardson and Moje (1999) suggest that if teachers can challenge a child's core understanding (as in Erin's case) rather than its 'peripheries' (as in Zane's case) they may have more chance of provoking change. In either case children need to recognise the data as anomalous for it to be effective and a plausible alternative explanation needs to be available to them. Some children (such as Grace), first need to be helped to clarify their own ideas before it is fruitful to provide the sorts of challenges illustrated.

So what can a primary teacher do if children are likely to respond in various ways? The challenge is not as daunting as it may seem. They can develop a classroom climate in which children are expected to think about their own ideas, to apply them to new situations and also to compare them with other children's ideas in class discussion. Children can be taught to listen to other viewpoints, weigh alternatives and evaluate their own ideas during group work. In science lessons, this will be linked with learning the use of evidence. In order to help children grasp abstract ideas in science, teachers may use story, drama and role-play, physical modelling, metaphors and analogies.

Analogies and electricity

In recent years there has been growing recognition that young children are in fact capable of reasoning by analogy. In support of the use of analogies it is argued that:

- **they can be powerful aids to explanation and understanding;**
- **they offer different means of communication;**

- **they may assist learners to rethink their own ideas;**
- **if several are available to the teacher there is an opportunity to select an appropriate one for a particular purpose;**
- **if learners create their own they may make their understanding explicit.**

The use of analogies and models is important in science not only to assist the learning but also to illustrate how science uses models. Teachers in primary schools have become increasingly aware of the range of analogies that can be drawn on (e.g. Asoko and de Bóo, 2001). Mulhall *et al.* (2001) point out that the abstract concepts of electricity are both intrinsically difficult to understand and also particularly dependent on models, analogies and metaphors. Studies on their use with primary pupils have been carried out by researchers, teachers and student teachers (e.g. Jabin and Smith, 1994; Newton and Newton, 1996). One of the analogies often used is to compare the flow of current in a circuit to water flow, sometimes with the use of a specially constructed physical model. Newton and Newton (1996) report how they used a soap dispenser and transparent tube to demonstrate flow to 6- and 7-year-olds, many of whom could then predict and explain the action of analogous electrical circuits in front of them. They quote a prolonged account by one individual (I = interviewer, C = child).

C: It's just … kind of … a bit like water. It's just going round and into the bulb.
I: What … the electricity's like water?
C: Yes.
I: How's the electricity like water?
C: Because, with the pump, you press that and the water goes round but that goes back into the bottle … like, say that was the light bulb and this was the battery. Press that … Right? And it would go all into the battery.
I: So what's happening to the electricity here?
C: The electricity's going through these wires … [*description of path of electricity*] … Electricity just looks invisible to us.
I: It does?
C: You see … with water … we can see the water as it moves along.
I: That's right.
C: With electricity, electricity's absolutely invisible to us.

They also add the caution that models may behave in ways unlike the electric circuit. Others too have underlined the value and the limitations of using models and analogies in teaching electricity, pointing out how examining where an analogy breaks down may also be a source of learning (Heywood and Parker, 1997). Drawing on a range of research, Mulhall *et al.* (2001) argue that:

> there are not even the beginnings of any form of justified consensus about the range and nature of models, and analogies and metaphors that might be appropriate for the teaching of electricity at any given level…

They say that teachers commonly adopt a single model, analogy or metaphor, largely based on personal preference for one that is then used as if just one will fit all possibilities. Primary teachers who deal with a diverse curriculum cannot be expected to have evaluated a wide range of models, analogies or metaphors for each scientific area they encounter. However, they can be alert to the possible strengths and weaknesses in any which they use or have recommended to them.

Pause for thought

Models, analogies and metaphors for electricity in circuits

A range of models, analogies and metaphors is used in teaching about electrical circuits. Each one has its own strengths. Having a class physically passing items round a circle may help young children understand the need for a circuit, while likening electricity to a central-heating water system may help older children think about continuous current flow round wires and components. However, each has its own weaknesses. People often point out that in the water system analogy, electricity does not emerge from a tap like water. What do you think are the strengths and weaknesses of the following:

- *children walking round the room in line?*
- *drawing circulating trucks which collect, carry and deliver loads representing energy?*
- *likening current flow to blood circulation round the body?*

Forces

An area of science that presents primary teachers with one of their greatest challenges is forces. In unpublished research among teachers attending courses of in-service training, the teaching of forces was identified as presenting the most difficulty (SHU, 2000). A study by Harlen *et al*. (1995) also identified teachers' lack of confidence in this area. Indeed, it is not only primary teachers who find the ideas underlying forces to be challenging. In March 2003, the *New Scientist* editorial discussed why even scientists use the 'hocus pocus' term 'centrifugal force' where no such force actually exists (*New Scientist*, 2003). *New Scientist* suggests that it is because subjective experience is overlaid on scientific judgement. When sunglasses slide off a car dashboard as a bend is taken too fast there appears to be a force pushing them even though there is no such force acting on the glasses at all. The article goes on to argue that our everyday experience of forces simply overwhelms the teaching of Newton's laws of motion. This supports the earlier view of Summers and Kruger (1992) who suggest that even after intensive teaching, students and teachers often revert to previously held non-scientific models to explain physical events.

It is unsurprising, given this lack of confidence about teaching forces, that student teachers on teaching placements are asked to teach forces disproportionately more often than any other area of science. Shallcross *et al*. (2002) report that, for example, trainees are ten times more likely to be asked to teach forces than Earth in space. It is likely that these topics are given to trainees because teachers find the underlying concepts very challenging. It may also be possible that trainees are teaching forces frequently, not because teachers are less confident teaching this subject, but because the topic of forces presents unrivalled opportunities for incorporating scientific enquiry into science learning (e.g. there are excellent opportunities for experimentation with relatively simple, but highly rewarding, items such as paper gliders and gyrocopters).

The apparent simplicity of an activity relating to forces occasionally hides problematical material. The often-taught activity of rolling cars down ramps does indeed make the collection and handling of data relatively easy and fruitful but it is also a minefield for the unwary who use it to try to explain the action of the force of gravity, friction or air resistance. Teachers who have used ramps and cars to try to explain gravity will know that it is not immediately apparent to all their children that the movement of a car along an inclined ramp is caused by the same force as that which makes objects fall straight down. Similarly, while allowing balls to fall and then measuring the height of bounce does produce interesting statistics, the underlying science is far from easy to explain (Figure 8.4).

Lauren
Bouncy ball experiment

Prediction

I think that the rubber ball will bounce the highest because it is less stiff than the tennis ball.

I will get the two balls and drop them off a table and see how high they bounce. This will give them the same amount of energy to start with.

	Tennis ball	Rubber ball
1st	13	19
2st	22	19
3st	24	20

The average is 19.3 cm for the rubber ball and the tennis ball was 19.6cm

I found out that the tennis ball was the most bouciest not the rubber ball. It is harder to measure them one at a time than when you roll them off together. When they dropped off together I could see that the tennis ball went highest each time. Measuring bounces is hard.

Figure 8.4. Report on bouncy ball experiment by Year 5 child

The concept of gravity

The force felt by us all the time is that of gravity. The history of understanding about gravity is long and fascinating (Galili, 2001) with the concepts of weight and gravitational force still offering many difficulties for educators. However, for primary science purposes the national requirements dictate that children should be taught that objects are pulled downwards because of gravitational attraction between them and the Earth. Also they should be taught how to measure forces and identify the directions in which they act. Teachers at Key Stages 1 and 2 will want to be secure in their own subject knowledge that:

- **gravity is the attraction between two masses;**
- **there is a distinction between mass and weight;**
- **weight is a result of gravity pulling on a mass;**
- **an object's weight is less on the Moon than on the Earth;**
- **gravity on Earth acts by pulling objects towards the middle of the Earth;**
- **the greater the distance between objects the less the gravitational attraction;**
- **the gravitational attraction of a massive object like the Earth extends far beyond the atmosphere, out into the far reaches of space;**
- **when drawing a force diagram larger forces are represented by longer arrows.**

In a study reported by Smith and Peacock (1992), primary teachers' ideas about the pull of the Earth were investigated prior to being taught about gravity. They were asked to predict what might happen when two masses (5 kg and 1 kg) were dropped simultaneously and from the same height – would one hit the ground before the other (Figure 8.5)? They also had to say which of these two masses is pulled harder by gravity. The correct answers are that they will fall at the same rate and hit the ground at the same time (ignoring air resistance which can be assumed to be negligible) but also that gravity pulls harder, five times harder, on the five kilogram mass than it does on the one kilogram mass. Most responded to the first question correctly but not to the second. What the teachers in the survey required to make sense of their ideas was the insight that large masses are pulled by gravity with a large force. The force of the pull is proportional to the mass. A mass five times bigger than another needs a pull five times larger to make it accelerate at the same rate as the smaller mass.

Figure 8.5. Drawing shown to teachers to elicit their ideas about gravity

The thread of inconsistent use of scientific ideas can also be followed in children's understanding about the force of gravity and the way it operates on objects. Russell *et al.* (1998) and Webb and Morrison (2000) confirm that children rarely use a consistently correct model when explaining gravity. In the latter study, Webb and Morrison reported that only 15% of Year 6 children use a consistent scientific model to explain the fall of objects such as balls to the centre of the Earth rather than simply downwards. Palmer (2001) confirmed this view in research which involved interviews with groups of children between 11 and 12 years of age. He showed them pictures and text about still and moving objects and asked them whether or not gravity was involved. Only 11% of respondents answered all correctly. While a very large majority agreed that gravity was operating on a person falling, only a small majority felt gravity operated on a buried brick.

Teaching about forces and gravity

If we are to teach about forces and gravity effectively, it is important to know about children's ideas in advance (Figure 8.6). However, as the majority of learners have highly inconsistent views about how the force of gravity operates, it is unlikely that we will find one teaching approach that will help all children to move towards scientifically accepted views. Teachers should offer children a wide variety of experience, discussion and direct teaching to help them clarify their ideas. When we teach about gravity we should take as many opportunities as possible to set it in a number of contexts. Here are just a few suggestions for setting gravity activities in a variety of contexts:

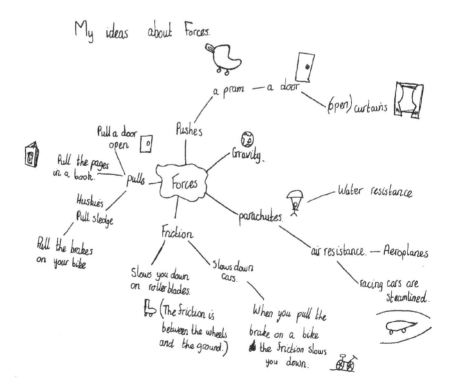

Figure 8.6. Children's ideas about gravity explored using a concept map in Year 5

- Children should be provided with the opportunity to discuss their experience of gravity pulling on masses. Children should hold masses of different size and discuss which is pulled harder by gravity. They should hang masses from elastic bands and springs and then discuss the stretching forces involved.

- In the last two years of primary education children should begin to weigh objects using spring balances calibrated in newtons. They should be encouraged to relate the greater pull in newtons to the strength of the pull of gravity on the object.

- Children should, at an early stage, have the opportunity to drop objects that are heavy for their size and compare the speed of fall. They should discuss the role of the pull of gravity in making them drop. At this stage we should avoid the use of objects that are light for their size as this brings in air resistance. This is discussed in the balanced and unbalanced forces section below.

- Teachers should emphasise that gravity pulls objects towards the centre of the Earth. Using miniature dolls and a globe it is possible to see that objects held on a string would hang 'down' from each doll's point of view wherever they are.

Conceptions about direction and size of forces

Current requirements indicate that children at Key Stage 2 should be taught:

- that friction, including air resistance, is a force which slows moving objects;
- that when objects are pushed or pulled an opposing pull or push is felt;
- how to measure forces and identify the direction in which they act.

Teachers will need to be clear in their own subject knowledge that when objects are stationary all the forces on them are balanced, when objects move at a constant speed in a straight line all the forces acting on them are balanced, and when objects accelerate or change direction unbalanced forces are operating on them. The possibilities for exciting teaching and learning expand when we bring in two or more forces. It is important to emphasise that although children's learning about abstract ideas is uneven, the topic is enjoyable and will stimulate the curiosity and understanding of learners (Figure 8.7).

The two forces of air resistance and gravity offer many opportunities for science investigations. Air resistance literally gets in the way of understanding gravity's simplicity. Without air resistance, all objects from feathers to hammers would fall at the same rate. Air resistance works more noticeably on objects, such as scraps of tissue paper, which are light for their size. The well known video clip of the astronaut Neil Armstrong dropping a feather and a hammer on the Moon is important viewing for all teachers of science as well as older children. Understanding that objects can be moving even though the forces of air resistance and gravity are balanced is difficult for many learners to accept. Most feel that there must be a larger force in the direction of movement (Osborne and Freyberg, 1985). Everyday experience does not lead learners to an understanding about terminal velocity.

Figure 8.7. Creative application of ideas about forces in Year 6 (from Vaz, 1998)

Even highly experienced teachers are prepared to admit to having difficulty under-standing the way that forces operate. Goldsworthy (1999) described the way in which she began to understand the forces involved in stopping her falling through the floor. She knew about gravity pulling her down but until she gave it thought and had the benefit of good teaching she found it difficult to accept that inanimate objects could exert a force pushing back against her. She talked about how she needed the evidence from the push back of a squashy balloon and a mind experiment with bendy planks of wood before she could accept that it was the distortion of the links between the molecules that led to the plank's ability to push back. For a fuller explanation about the strength and flexibility of materials see Gordon (1976).

Teaching about the direction and size of forces

Children need experiences that prompt them to experiment with and make sense of the direction and relative size of forces. Russell *et al*. (1998) suggest that there are strong positive reasons why primary teachers should formally teach the conventions associated with the use of arrows:

- arrows show the direction of a force;
- the longer the arrow the greater the force;
- where arrows oppose each other and are equal the forces on the object are balanced so an object is either stationary or moving at a constant speed.

Pause for thought

Pushing back

Parker and Heywood (2000) asked a number of qualified teachers and student teachers about their understanding of the forces involved in floating and sinking. When pushing a balloon into a tank of water only approximately 10% of the respondents used technical terms such as upthrust. Even fewer respondents offered explanations that involved the volume of water being displaced and the effect this has on the force of upthrust.

Carry out this 'simple' investigation for yourselves. What do you see? What do you feel? Can you make the link between pushing down on the balloon, the rise in water level, and the size of the upthrust felt? How might you use and extend this information to help children explain floating and sinking in Key Stage 1 and Key Stage 2?

Teaching about the size and direction of force should use as many opportunities as possible to set it in a number of contexts.

- Very young children can be asked to talk about large and small pushes or pulls. Ask them to draw a car moving with a big push and compare that with a car being moved with a small push.
- Children should be given the task of seeing which objects can be moved with the small force of blowing, the larger force of pushing with a straw, and the bigger force of pushing with a rolled up sheet of paper.
- Give the children instances such as an ant pushing a tiny stone, a child kicking a ball, an adult pushing over a tree, and a bulldozer demolishing a wall. Discuss and draw the size and direction of these forces.
- Ensure that children of all ages get the chance to experiment with the push back from water and the forces on a floating object. Weighing in air and in water

challenges children to think about the pull of gravity and the push back of upthrust from the water.

- Children can experiment with the gravitational pull on a helium balloon by adding paperclips to it.
- Discuss what happens when very light objects, such as pieces of tissue or cotton wool, fall and reach their terminal velocity.

Physical processes:

a summary of key points

Physical processes are now well established in the primary curriculum but some ideas about electricity and forces may be hard to learn and challenging to teach. However, related activities can be motivating and can engage children as active learners. Children will have had many experiences of electricity and forces out of school and they will have formed ideas that will influence how they make sense of what is taught. Teachers need to know about the sorts of alternative ideas that learners may already hold and have strategies available for challenging how they think. Practical activity is important but not sufficient on its own. This needs to be accompanied by other approaches including talking, drawing, modelling, the use of analogies and effective exposition. Teachers may also have to check their own knowledge and understanding of key ideas before teaching about electricity or forces.

Abd-El-Khalick, F. and Lederman, N. (2000) Improving science teachers' conceptions of the nature of science: a critical review of the literature, *International Journal of Science Education*, 22(7), 665–702.

Alters, B. (1997a) Whose nature of science? *Journal of Research in Science Teaching*, 34(1), 39–56.

Alters, B. (1997b) Nature of science: a diversity or uniformity of ideas? *Journal of Research in Science Teaching*, 34(10), 1105–8.

Appleton, K. and Asoko, H. (1996) A case study of a teacher's progress toward using a constructivist view of learning to inform teaching in elementary science, *Science Teacher Education*, 80(2), 165–80.

Asoko, H. and de Bóo, M. (2001) *Analogies and Illustrations: Representing Ideas in Primary Science*. Hatfield: Association for Science Education.

Bar, V. and Galili, I. (1994) Stages of children's views about evaporation, *International Journal of Science Education*, 16(2), 157–74.

Bar, V. and Travis, A. (1991) Children's views concerning phase changes, *Journal of Research in Science Teaching*, 28(4), 363–82.

Barker, M. (1995) A plant is an animal standing on its head, *Journal of Biological Education*, 29(30), 201–8.

Barker, M. and Carr, M. (1989) Teaching and learning about photosynthesis. Part I: An assessment in terms of students' prior knowledge, *International Journal of Science Education*, 11(1), 49–56.

Bartholomew, H., Osborne, J. and Ratcliffe, M. (2004) Teaching pupils 'ideas-about-science': five dimensions of effective practice, *Science Education*.

Baxter, J. (1989) Children's understanding of familiar astronomical events, *International Journal of Science Education*, 11 (special issue), 502–13.

Bell, B. (1981) When is an animal not an animal? *Journal of Biological Education*, 15(3), 213–18.

Bell, B. and Barker, M. (1982) Towards a scientific concept of animal, *Journal of Biological Education*, 16(3), 197–200.

Black, P. (1995) 1987 to 1995 – the struggle to formulate a National Curriculum for science in England and Wales, *Studies in Science Education*, 26, 159–88.

Black, P. and Harlen, W. (1993) How can we specify concepts for primary science? in P. J. Black and A. M. Lucas (eds), *Children's Informal Ideas in Science*. London: Routledge, 208–29.

Blanco, A. and Prieto, T. (1997) Pupils' views on how stirring and temperature affect the dissolution of a solid in a liquid: a cross age study (12–18), *International Journal of Science Education*, 19(3), 303–15.

Bonnett, M. and Williams, J. (1998) Environmental education and primary children's attitudes towards nature and the environment, *Cambridge Journal of Education*, 28(2), 159–74.

Braund, M. (1998) Trends in children's concepts of vertebrate and invertebrate, *Journal of Biological Education*, 32(2), 112–18.

Campanario, J. M. (2002) The parallelism between scientists' and students' resistance to new scientific ideas, *International Journal of Science Education*, 24(10), 1095–110.

Carré, C. and Carter, D. (1990) Primary teachers' self perceptions concerning implementation of the National Curriculum for science in the UK, *International Journal of Science Education*, 12(4), 324–41.

Carré, C. and Carter, D. (1993) Primary teachers' self-perceptions concerning implementation of the National Curriculum for science in the UK – revisited, *International Journal of Science Education*, 15(4), 457–70.

Chalmers, A. F. (1978) *What Is This Thing Called Science?* Milton Keynes: Open University Press.

Chambers, D. W. (1983) Stereotypic images of the scientist: the Draw-a-Scientist Test. *Science Education*, 67, 255–65.

Chapman, B. (1994) The overselling of science education in the 1980s, in R. Levinson (ed.), *Teaching Science*. London: Routledge.

Children's Learning in Science (CLIS) (1987) *Children's Learning in Science Project – CLIS in the Classroom*. Leeds: Centre for Science and Mathematics Study, University of Leeds.

Children's Learning in Science Project (various 1988–1992) *Children's Learning in Science Project (CLIS)*. Centre for Studies in Science and Mathematics Education, University of Leeds.

Cooper, G. (1994) The role of outdoor education in education for the 21st century, *Environmental Education*, 46 (Summer), 28–31.

Cotham, J. and Smith, E. (1981) Development and validation of the conceptions of scientific theories test, *Journal of Research in Science Teaching*, 18, 387–96.

Cuthbert, A. J. (2000) Do children have a holistic view of their internal body maps? *School Science Review*, 82(299), 25–32.

Daehler, K. R. and Shinohara, M. (2001) A complete circuit is a complete circle: exploring the potential of case materials and methods to develop teachers' content knowledge and pedagogical content knowledge of science, *Research in Science Education*, 31(2), 267–88.

Dagher, Z. R. (1994) Does the use of analogies contribute to conceptual change? *Science Education*, 78(6), 601–14.

Dearing, R. (1993) *The National Curriculum and Its Assessment: Final Report*. London: SCAA.

Department for Education/Welsh Office (1995) *Science in the National Curriculum*. London. HMSO.

Department for Education and Employment (DfEE) (1998) *Initial Teacher Training National Curriculum for Primary Science: Annex E of DfEE Circular 4/98 (revised September 2000)*. London: Teacher Training Agency.

Department for Education and Employment/Qualifications and Curriculum Authority (DfEE/QCA) (1998) *Science: Teacher's Guide: A Scheme of Work for Key Stages 1 and 2*. London: HMSO.

Department for Education and Employment/Qualifications and Curriculum Authority (DfEE/QCA) (1999) *Science: The National Curriculum for England*. London: HMSO.

Department for Education and Skills/Teacher Training Agency (DfES/TTA) (2002) *Qualifying to Teach: Professional Standards for Qualified Teacher Status and Requirements for Initial Teacher Training*. London: Teacher Training Agency.

Department of Education and Science (1978) *Primary Education in England: A Survey by HM Inspectors of Schools*. London: HMSO.

Department of Education and Science (1983) *Science in Primary Schools: A Discussion Paper Produced by the HMI Science Committee*. London: HMSO.

Department of Education and Science (1989) *The Curriculum from 5–16: Curriculum Matters 2*. London: HMSO.

Department of Education and Science/Welsh Office (1985) *Science 5–16: A Statement of Policy*. London: HMSO.

Department of Education and Science/Welsh Office (1989) *Science in the National Curriculum*. London: HMSO.

Department of Education and Science/Welsh Office (1991) *Science in the National Curriculum*. London: HMSO.

Diakidoy, I. N. and Kendeou, P. (2001) Facilitating conceptual change in astronomy: a comparison of the effectiveness of two instructional approaches, *Learning and Instruction*, 11, 1–20.

Dickinson, D. K. (1987) The development of a concept of material kind, *Science Education*, 71(4), 615–28.

Driver, R. (1985) Beyond appearances: the conservation of matter under physical and chemical transformation, in R. Driver, E. Guesne and A. Tiberghien (eds), *Children's Ideas in Science*. Milton Keynes: Open University Press, 145–69.

Driver, R. and Bell, B. (1986) Students' thinking and the learning of science, *School Science Review*, 67, 443–56.

Driver, R., Guesne, E. and Tiberghien, A. (eds) (1985) *Children's Ideas in Science*. Milton Keynes: Open University Press.

Driver, R., Squires, A, Rushworth, P. and Wood-Robinson, V. (eds) (1994a) *Making Sense of Secondary Science*. London: Routledge.

Driver, R., Asoko, H., Leach, J., Mortimer, E. and Scott, P. (1994b) Constructing scientific knowledge in the classroom, *Educational Researcher*, 23(7), 5–12.

Driver, R., Leach, J., Millar, R. and Scott, P. (1996) *Young People's Images of Science*. Buckingham: Open University Press.

Duit, R. (2003) *Students' and Teachers' Conceptions and Science Education (STCSE): Bibliography*. Available online at: *http://www.ipn.un-kiel.de/aktuell/stcse/stcse.html*.

Dunbar, R. (1995) *The Trouble with Science*. London: Faber.

Duschl, R. A. and Wright, E. (1989) A case study of high school teachers' decision-making models for planning and teaching science, *Journal of Research in Science Teaching*, 26, 467–501.

Eagles, P. F. J. and Demare, R. (1999) Factors influencing children's environmental attitudes, *Journal of Environmental Education*, 30(4), 33–7.

Egan, B., Marsh, G. and Parkes, T. (2003) A changing environment – children's ideas, *Primary Science Review*, 76, 21–4.

Feasey, R. (ed.) (2001) *Science Is Like a Tub of Ice Cream: Cool and Fun*. Hatfield: Association for Science Education.

Feasey, R. and Siraj-Blatchford, J. (1998) *Key Skills and Communication*. Durham University and Tyneside TEC.

Fensham, P. J., Gunstone, R. F. and White, R. T. (1994) Science content and constructivist views of learning and teaching, in P. Fensham, R. Gunstone and R. White (eds), *The Content of Science: A Constructivist Approach to Its Teaching and Learning*. London: Falmer, 1–8.

Fox, R. (2001) Constructivism examined, *Oxford Review of Education*, 27(1), 23–35.

Galili, I. (2001) Weight versus gravitational force: historical and educational perspectives, *International Journal of Science Education*, 23, 1073–93.

Gamache, P. (2002) University students as creators of personal knowledge: an alternative epistemological view, *Teaching in Higher Education*, 7(3), 277–294.

Gilbert, J. K., Boulter, C. and Rutherford, M. (1988a) Models in explanations, Part I: Horses for courses? *International Journal of Science Education*, 20(1), 83–97.

Goldsworthy, A. (1999) But tables can't push, *Primary Science Review*, 58, 10–11.

Goldsworthy, A. (2000) *Investigations: Making an Impact*. Hatfield: Association for Science Education.

Goldsworthy, A., Feasey, R. and Ball, S. (1997) *Making Sense of Primary Science Investigations*. Hatfield: Association for Science Education.

Goldsworthy, A., Watson, R. and Wood-Robinson, V. (1999a) *Investigations: Getting to Grips with Graphs*. Hatfield: Association for Science Education.

Goldsworthy, A., Watson, R. and Wood-Robinson, V. (1999b) *Investigations: Developing Understanding*. Hatfield: Association for Science Education.

Goldsworthy, A., Watson, R. and Wood-Robinson, V. (2000) *Developing Understanding in Scientific Enquiry*. Hatfield: Association for Science Education.

Gordon, J. (1976) *The New Science of Strong Materials*. London: Pelican.

Gott, R., Duggan, S. and Roberts, R. (2003) *Research into Understanding Scientific Evidence*. Available online at: *www.dur.ac.uk/richard.gott/Evidence/cofev.htm* (in progress).

Grace, M. and Byrne, J. (2003) Teaching environmental education in primary and secondary schools through collaborative community projects: benefits and barriers, *Environmental Education*, 72, 26–9.

Grace, M. and Sharp, J. (2000) Young people's views on the importance of conserving biodiversity, *School Science Review*, 82(298), 49–56.

Harlen, W. (1978) Does content matter in primary science? *School Science Review*, 59, 614–25.

Harlen, W. (1992a) Research and the development of science in the primary school, *International Journal of Science Education*, 14(5), 491–503.

Harlen, W. (1992b) *The Teaching of Science*. London: David Fulton.

Harlen, W. (1998) The last ten years; the next ten years, in R. Sherrington (ed.), *ASE Guide to Primary Science Education*. Hatfield: Association for Science Education.

Harlen, W. (2000) *Teaching, Learning and Assessing Science 5–12*, London: Paul Chapman.

Harlen, W. (2000) *The Teaching of Science in Primary Schools*. London: David Fulton.

Harlen, W. and Holroyd, C. (1997) Primary teachers' understanding of concepts of science: impact on confidence and teaching, *International Journal of Science Education*, 19(1), 93–105.

Harlen, W., Holroyd, C. and Byrne, M. (1995) *Confidence and Understanding in Teaching Science and Technology in Primary Schools*, Scottish Council for Research in Education, Research Report 65. Edinburgh: SCRE.

Harrison, A. G. and Treagust, D. F. (2000) A typology of school science models, *International Journal of Science Education*, 22(9), 1011–26.

Hatzinikita, V. and Koulaidis, V. (1997) Pupils' ideas on conservation during changes in the state of water, *Research in Science and Technological Education*, 15(1), 53–70.

Hellden, G. (1996) Elements in pupils' ideas about ecological processes, in A. Giordan and Y. Girault (eds), *The New Learning Models. Their Consequences for the Teaching of Biology, Health and Environment*. Nice: Z'editions, 142–154.

Heywood, D. and Parker, J. (1997) Confronting the analogy: primary teachers exploring the usefulness of analogies in the teaching and learning of electricity, *International Journal of Science Education*, 19(8), 869–85.

Heywood, D. and Parker, J. (2001) Describing the cognitive landscape in learning and teaching about forces, *International Journal of Science Education*, 23(11), 1177–99.

Hodson, D. (1998) *Teaching and Learning Science: Towards a Personalised Approach*. Buckingham: Open University Press.

Holding, B. (1987) 'Investigation of School Children's Understanding of the Process of Dissolving with Special Reference to the Conservation of Matter and the Development of Atomistic Ideas'. Unpublished PhD thesis, University of Leeds.

Hollins, M. and Whitby, V. (2001) *Progression in Primary Science: A Guide to the Nature and Practice of Primary Science at Key Stages 1 and 2*. London: David Fulton.

Jabin, Z. and Smith, R. G. (1994) Using analogies of electricity flow in circuits to improve understanding, *Primary Science Review*, 35, 23–6.

Jarvis, J., McKeon, F. and Taylor, N. (2002) *Promoting Conceptual Change through Group Discussion of Thought Provoking Science Problems*. Paper presented at the BERA Conference, September 2002.

Jarvis, T., Pell, A. and McKeon, F. (2003) Changes in primary teachers' science knowledge and understanding during a two-year in-service programme, *Research in Science and Technological Education*, 21(1), 17–42.

Jarvis, T., McKeon, F., Coates, D. and Vause, J. (2001) Beyond generic mentoring: helping trainee teachers to teach primary science, *Research in Science and Technological Education*, 19(1), 5–23.

Jenkins, E. W. (1995) Central policy and teacher response: scientific investigation in the National Curriculum of England and Wales, *International Journal of Science Education*, 17(4), 471–80.

Jewell, N. (2002) Examining children's models of seed, *Journal of Biological Education*, 36(3), 116–22.

Johnsey, R., Peacock, G., Sharp, J. and Wright, D. (2002) *Primary Science Knowledge and Understanding*. Exeter: Learning Matters.

Johnson, P. (1998a) Progression in children's understanding of a 'basic' particle theory: a longitudinal study, *International Journal of Science Education*, 20(4), 393–412.

Johnson, P. (1998b) Children's understanding of changes of state involving the gas state, Part 1: boiling water and the particle theory, *International Journal of Science Education*, 20(5), 567–83.

Johnson, P. (1998c) Children's understanding of changes of state involving the gas state, Part 2: evaporation and condensation below boiling point, *International Journal of Science Education*, 20(6), 695–709.

Johnson, P. (2000) Children's understanding of substances, Part 1: recognizing chemical change, *International Journal of Science Education*, 22(7), 719–37.

Johnson, P. (2002) Children's understanding of substances, Part 2: explaining chemical change, *International Journal of Science Education*, 24(10), 1037–54.

Jones, B. L., Lynch, P. P. and Reesink, C. (1987) Children's conceptions of the Earth, Sun and Moon, *International Journal of Science Education*, 9(1), 43–53.

Kelly, A. V. (1999) *The Curriculum: Theory and Practice*. London: Paul Chapman.

Keogh, B. and Naylor, S. (1997) *Starting Points for Science*. Sandbach: Millgate House.

Keogh, B., Naylor, S., de Bóo, M. and Barnes, J. (2002) *Primary Science: PGCE Professional Workbook*. Exeter: Learning Matters.

Kibble, B. (2002) How do you picture electricity? *Primary Science Review*, 74, 28–30.

Kikas, E. (1998) The impact of teaching on students' definitions and explanations of astronomical phenomena, *Learning and Instruction*, 8(5), 439–54.

Klein, C. (1982) Children's concepts of the Earth and the Sun: a cross cultural study, *Science Education*, 65(1), 95–107.

Krnel D., Watson, R. and Glazer, S. A. (1998) Survey of research related to the development of the concept of 'matter', *International Journal of Science Education*, 20(3), 257–89.

Kruger, C. and Summers, M. (1989) Some primary teachers' understanding of changes in materials, *School Science Review*, 71(255), 17–27.

Lantz, O. and Kass, H. (1987) Chemistry teachers' functional paradigms, *Science Education*, 71, 117–34.

Leach, J. and Scott, P. (2003) Individual and sociocultural views of learning in science education, *Science and Education*, 12, 91–113.

Lederman, N. and Abd-El-Khalick, F. (1998) Avoiding the de-natured science: activities that promote understandings of the nature of science, in W. F. McComas (ed.), *The Nature of Science in Science Education: Rationales and Strategies*. Dordrecht: Kluwer, 83–126.

Lederman, N. and O'Malley, M. (1990) Students' perceptions of tentativeness in science: development, use, and sources of change, *Science Education*, 74, 225–39.

Limón, M. and Mason, L. (2002) *Reconsidering Conceptual Change. Issues in Theory and Practice*. Dordrecht: Kluwer Academic Press.

Longdon, K., Black, P. and Solomon, J. (1991) Children's interpretation of dissolving, *International Journal of Science Education*, 13(1), 59–68.

Loughran, J. J. (2002) Effective reflective practice: in search of meaning in learning about teaching, *Journal of Teacher Education*, 53(1), 33–43.

Lunn, S. (2002) 'What we think we can safely say ...': primary teachers' views of the nature of science, *British Educational Research Journal*, 28(5), 649–70.

McComas, W. F. (1998) The principal elements of the nature of science: dispelling the myths, in W. F. McComas (ed.) *The Nature of Science in Science Education: Rationales and Strategies*. Dordecht: Kluwer, 53–70.

McComas, W. F. and Olsen J. (1998) The Nature of Science in International Science Education Standards Documents, in W. F. McComas (ed.) *The Nature of Science in Science Education: Rationales and Strategies*. Dordecht: Kluwer, 41–52.

McGuigan, L. (2000) Origins and transformations of materials – developing understanding, *Primary Science Review*, 63.

Millar, R. (1989) Constructive criticisms, *International Journal of Science Education*, 11, 587–96.

Millar, R. and Osborne, J. (1998) *Beyond 2000: Science Education for the Future – A Report with Ten Recommendations*. London: King's College.

Moon, B. (1994) The National Curriculum: origins, context and implications, in A. Pollard and J. Bourne (eds), *Teaching and Learning in the Primary School*. Milton Keynes: Open University Press.

Morris, M. and Schagen, I. (1996) *Green Attitudes or Learned Responses?* Slough, Berkshire: NFER Global Environmental Education.

Mulhall, P., McKittrick, B. and Gunstone, R. (2001) A perspective on the resolution of confusions in the teaching of electricity, *Research in Science Education*, 31, 575–87.

Naylor, S. and Keogh, B. (2000) *Concept Cartoons in Education*. Sandbach: Millgate House.

New Scientist (2003) The word: centrifugal, *New Scientist*, 1 March, 47.

Newton, L. D. (2001) Teaching for understanding in primary science, *Evaluation and Research in Education*, 15(3), 143–53.

Newton, L. and Newton, D. (1996) Young children and understanding electricity, *Primary Science Review*, 41, 14–16.

Newton, L. D and Newton, D. P. (1998) Primary children's conceptions about science and scientists, *International Journal of Science Education*, 20(9), 1137–49.

Nott, M. and Wellington, J. (1993) Your nature of science profile: an activity for science teachers, *School Science Review*, 75(270), 109–12.

Nuffield Primary Science (1995) *Teachers' Guides*. London: Collins Educational.

Nussbaum, J. (1985) The Earth as a cosmic body, in R. Driver, E. Guesne and A. Tiber-ghien (eds), *Children's Ideas in Science*. Milton Keynes: Open University Press.

Oakley, D. (1993) A National Curriculum for science, in R. Sherrington (ed.), *ASE Science Teachers' Handbook (Primary)*. Trowbridge: Redwood.

Office for Standards in Education (OFSTED) (1999) *Primary Review 1994–1998* London: HMSO.

Office for Standards in Education (OFSTED) (2001) *Subject Reports 2000/2001*. Available online at: *www.ofsted.gov.uk/publications/*.

Osborne, J. and Simon, S. (1996) Primary science: past and future directions, *Studies in Science Education*, 26, 99–147.

Osborne, J., Wadsworth, P. and Black, P. (1992) *Processes of Life: Primary Space Project*. Liverpool: Liverpool University Press.

Osborne, J., Black, P., Smith, M. and Meadows, J. (1990) *Light*, SPACE Project Research Report. Liverpool: Liverpool University Press.

Osborne, J., Wadsworth, P., Black, P. and Meadows, J. (1994) *The Earth in Space*, SPACE Project Research Report. Liverpool: Liverpool University Press.

Osborne, J., Ratcliffe, M., Collins, S., Millar, R. and Duschl, R. (2001) *What Should We Teach about Science? A Delphi Study*. London: King's College.

Osborne, J., Collins, S., Ratcliffe, M., Millar, R. and Duschl, R. (2003) What 'ideas-about-science' should be taught in school science? A Delphi study of the expert community, *Journal of Research in Science Teaching*, 40(7), 692–720.

Osborne, R. and Cosgrove, M. (1983) Children's conceptions of the changes of state of water, *Journal of Research in Science Teaching*, 20(9), 825–38.

Osborne, R.J. and Freyberg, P. (1985) *Learning in Science: The Implications of Children's Science*. London: Heinemann.

Oversby, J. (2000) Good explanations for dissolving, *Primary Science Review*, 63, 16–19.

Palmer, D. (2001) Students' alternative conceptions and scientifically acceptable conceptions about gravity, *International Journal of Science Education*, 23, 691–706.

Palmer, J. A. and Neal, P. (1994) *The Handbook of Environmental Education*. London: Routledge.

Parker, J. (1995) Words on paper, *Primary Science Review*, 36, 18–22.

Parker, J. and Heywood, D. (1996) Circuit training – working towards the notion of a complete circuit, *Primary Science Review*, 41, 16–19.

Parker, J. and Heywood, D. (2000) Exploring the relationship between subject knowledge and pedagogical content knowledge in primary teachers' learning about forces, *International Journal of Science Education*, 22(1), 89–111.

Parker, J. and Spink, E. (1997) Becoming science teachers: an evaluation of the initial stages of primary teacher training, *Assessment and Evaluation in Higher Education*, 22(1), 17–31.

Peacock, G. (1998) *Science for Primary Teachers*. London: Letts.

Pendlington, S., Palacio, D. and Summers, M. (1993) *Understanding Materials and Why They Change*. Oxford: Primary School Teachers and Science (PSTS) Project, Oxford University Department of Educational Studies and Westminster College.

Poulson, L. (2001) Paradigm lost? Subject knowledge, primary teachers and education policy, *British Journal of Educational Studies*, 49(1), 40–55.

Primary School Teachers and Science Project (PSTS) (1988–1993) *Working Papers 1–17*. Oxford: Oxford University/Westminster College.

Qualifications and Curriculum Authority (2002) *Implications for Teaching and Learning from the 2002 Tests*. Available online at: www.qca.org.uk/ca/tests. London: QCA .

Qualifications and Curriculum Authority/Department for Education and Employment (1998, with amendments 2000) *Science: A Scheme of Work for Key Stages 1 and 2*. London: QCA.

Ratcliffe, M. (1999) Evaluation of abilities in interpreting media reports of scientific research, *International Journal of Science Education*, 21(10), 1085–99.

Reiss, M.J. et al. (2002) An international study of young peoples' drawings of what is inside themselves, *Journal of Biological Education*, 36(2), 58–64.

Ritchie, R. (1996) Science in the National Curriculum, in D. Coulby and S. Ward (eds), *The Primary Core Curriculum: Policy into Practice*. London: Cassell.

Russell, T. and Watt, D. (1990) *Growth*, SPACE Project Research Report. Liverpool: Liverpool University Press.

Russell, T., Longden, K. and McGuigan, L. (1991) *Materials*, Primary SPACE Project Research Report. Liverpool: Liverpool University Press.

Russell, T., Longden, K, and McGuigan, L. (1998) *Forces*, Primary SPACE Project Research Report. Liverpool: Liverpool University Press.

Russell, T., Qualter, A. and McGuigan, L. (1994) *Evaluation of the Implementation of Science in the National Curriculum (Volumes 1, 2 and 3)*. London: School Curriculum and Assessment Authority.

Russell, T., Qualter, A. and McGuigan, L. (1995) Reflections on the implementation of National Curriculum science policy for the 5–14 age range: findings and interpretations from a national evaluation study in England, *International Journal of Science Education*, 17(4), 481–92.

Schneekloth, L.H. (1989) Where did you go? The forest. What did you see? Nothing, *Children's' Environments Quarterly*, 6(1), 14–17.

Science Processes and Concept Exploration (SPACE) (1990–1998) *Research Reports* (various). Liverpool: Liverpool University Press.

Selley, N. (2000) Students' spontaneous use of a particulate model for dissolution, *Research in Science Education*, 30(4), 389–402.

Shallcross, T., Spink, E., Stephenson, P. and Warwick, P. (2002) How primary trainee teachers perceive the development of their own scientific knowledge: links between confidence, content and competence? *International Journal of Science Education*, 24(12), 1293–312.

Sharp, J. G. (1995) Children's astronomy: implications for curriculum developments at Key Stage 1 and the future of infant science in England and Wales, *International Journal of Early Years Education*, 3(3), 17–49.

Sharp, J. G. (1996) Children's astronomical beliefs: a preliminary study of Year 6 children in south-west England, *International Journal of Science Education*, 18(6), 685–712.

Sharp, J. G. (1999) Young children's ideas about the Earth in space, *International Journal of Early Years Education*, 7(2), 159–72.

Sharp, J. and Byrne, J. (2003) *Primary Science: Audit and Test. Assessing Your Knowledge and Understanding*. Exeter: Learning Matters.

Sharp, J., Peacock, G., Johnsey, R., Simon, S. and Smith, R. (2002) *Primary Science: Teaching Theory and Practice*. Exeter: Learning Matters.

Sheffield Hallam University (SHU) (2000) *Teachers' Ideas About Forces*. Internal report (unpublished).

Shepardson, D. P. (2002) Bugs, butterflies, and spiders: children's understanding about insects, *International Journal of Science Education*, 24(6), 627–43.

Shepardson, D. P. and Moje, E. J. (1999) The role of anomalous data in restructuring fourth graders' frameworks for understanding electric circuits, *International Journal of Science Education*, 21(1), 77–94.

Shipstone, D. M. (1985) Electricity in simple circuits, in R. Driver, E. Guesne and A. Tiberghien (eds), *Children's Ideas in Science*. Milton Keyes: Open University Press, 33–51.

Shulman, L. S. (1986) Those who understand: knowledge growth in teaching, *Educational Researcher*, 15(2), 4–14.

Smith, D. C. and Neale, D. C. (1991) The construction of subject-matter knowledge in primary science teaching, in J. Brophy (ed.), *Advances in Research on Teaching*. Greenwich: JAI Press.

Smith, M. U., Lederman, N. G., Bell, R. L., McComas, W. F. and Clough, M. P. (1997) How great is the disagreement about the nature of science? A response to Alters, *Journal of Research in Science Teaching*, 34(10), 1101–4.

Smith, R. and Peacock, G. (1992) Tackling contradictions in teachers' understanding of gravity and air resistance, *Evaluation and Research in Education*, 6(2&3), 113–28.

Sneider, C. and Ohady, M. M. (1998) Unravelling students' misconceptions about the Earth's shape and gravity, *Science Education*, 82(2), 265–84.

Solomon, J. (1986) Children's explanations, *Oxford Review of Education*, 12(1), 41–55.

Solomon, J. (1994) The rise and fall of constructivism, *Studies in Science Education*, 23, 1–19.

Stavy, R and Stachel, D. (1985) Children's ideas about 'solid' and 'liquid', *European Journal of Science Education*, 7(4), 407–21.

Summers, M. (1994) Science in the primary school: the problem of teachers' curricular expertise, *The Curriculum Journal*, 5(2), 179–93.

Summers, M. and Kruger, C. (1993) *A Longitudinal Study of the Development of Primary School Teachers' Understanding of Force and Energy.* Oxford: PSTS.

Summers, M. and Kruger, C. (1994) A longitudinal study of a constructivist approach to improving primary teachers' subject matter knowledge in science, *Teaching and Teacher Education*, 10(5), 499–519.

Sungur, S., Tekkaya, C. and Geban, O. (2001) The contribution of conceptual; change texts accompanied by concept mapping to students understanding of the human circulatory system, *School Science and Mathematics*, 10(2), 91–101.

Sutton, C. (1992) *Words, Science and Learning.* Open University Press: Buckingham.

Tamir, P., Gal-Choppin, R. and Nussinovitz, R. (1981) How do intermediate and junior high school students conceptualize living and nonliving? *Journal of Research in Science Teaching*, 18, 241–8.

Tao, P. and Gunstone, R. F. (2000) The process of conceptual change in forces and motion during computer supported physics instruction, *Journal of Research in Science and Technology*, 36(7), 859–82.

Teacher Training Agency (2002) *Qualifying to Teach. Handbook of Guidance.* London: Teacher Training Agency.

Tunnicliffe, S. D. (2001) Talking about plants – comments of primary school groups looking at plant exhibits in a botanical garden, *Journal of Biological Education*, 36(1), 27–34.

Tunnicliffe, S. D. and Reiss, M. J. (1999a) Building a model of the environment: how do children see animals? *Journal of Biological Education*, 33(3), 142–8.

Tunnicliffe, S. D. and Reiss, M. J. (1999b) Student's understandings about animal skeletons, *International Journal of Science Education*, 21(11), 1187–200.

Tunnicliffe, S. D. and Reiss, M. J. (2000) Building a model of the environment: how do children see plants? *Journal of Biological Education*, 34(4), 172–7.

Trowbridge, J. E. and Mintzes, J. J. (1985) Students alternative conceptions of animals and animal classification, *School Science and Mathematics*, 85(4), 304–16.

Tytler, R. (2000) A comparison of Year 1 and Year 6 students' conceptions of evaporation and condensation: dimensions of conceptual progression, *International Journal of Science Education*, 22(5), 447–67.

Van Matre, S. (1990) *Earth Education: A New Beginning.* Greenville, W.Va.: Institute for Earth Education.

Vaz, S. (1998) Sam feels the force, *Primary Science.* Hatfield: Association for Science Education.

Vickery, D. (1995) The case for more evidence to substantiate statutory curriculum proposals, *Primary Science Review*, 38, 4–5.

Vosniadou, S. (1991) Designing curricula for conceptual restructuring: lessons from the study of knowledge acquisition in astronomy, *Journal of Curriculum Studies*, 23(3), 219–37.

Vosniadou, S. (1994) Capturing and modelling the process of conceptual change, *Learning and Instruction*, 4, 45–69.

Vosniadou, S. and Brewer, W. F. (1992) Mental models of the Earth: a study of conceptual change in childhood, *Cognitive Psychology*, 24, 535–85.

Vosniadou, S. and Brewer, W. F. (1994) Mental models of the day/night cycle, *Cognitive Science*, 18, 123–83.

Vygotsky, L. S (1978) *Mind in Society: The Development of Higher Psychological Processes.* Cambridge, MA: Harvard University Press.

Wandersee, J. H and Shussler, E. E. (2001) Toward a theory of plant blindness, *Plant Science*, 47(1), 2–9.

Warwick, P. and Sparkes-Linfield, R. (1996) Speeding up plant growth and children's ideas, *Primary Science Review*, 43, 23–9.

Watt, D. (1998) Children's learning of science concepts, in R. Sherrington (ed.), *ASE Guide to Primary Science Education*. Hatfield: Association for Science Education, 51–62.

Watt, D. and Russell, T. (1990) *Sound*, SPACE Project Research Report. Liverpool: Liverpool University Press.

Watts, M. and Bentley, D. (1994) Humanising and feminising school science: reviving anthropomorphic and animistic thinking in constructivist science education, *International Journal of Science Education*, 16(1), 83–97.

Webb, L. and Morrison, I. (2000) Children's conceptions about the Earth, *School Science Review*, 81(296), 99–103.

Wertsch, J. V. (1991) *Voices of the Mind: A Sociocultural Approach to Mediated Action*. Hemel Hempstead: Harvester Wheatsheaf.

White, R. and Gunstone, R. (1992) *Probing Understanding*. London: Falmer.

Wildy, H. and Wallace, J. (1995) Understanding teaching or teaching for understanding: alternative frameworks for science classrooms, *Journal of Research in Science Teaching*, 32, 143–56.

Wragg, E. C., Bennett, S. N. and Carré, C. G. (1989) Primary teachers and the national curriculum, *Research Papers in Education*, 4(3), 17–45.